The Bluest Eye

A Reader's Companion

Toni Morrison's

The Bluest Eye

A Reader's Companion

Edited by
Protibha Mukherjee Sahukar

Asia Book Club

an international publishing house

Published by

Asia Book Club

C 3/1, Janakpuri
New Delhi 110 058
Ph. 9818755529
email: prestigebooks@gmail.com
website: asiabookclub.com
ISBN: 81-7851-048-0

Printed at Chaman Offset Press, New Delhi 110 002

Contents

Preface

The Bluest Eye (1970) is the novel that launched Toni Morrison into the limelight as a gifted African American writer. She is one of the most celebrated black writers and is recognized as a major figure in American literature.

The Bluest Eye is an artistic portrayal of the harsh realities facing Pecola Breedlove struggling to make her way through an unforgiving white world. She is a lonely black girl who yearns for blue eyes as those eyes are a representation of what is best in the world. She imagines that blue eyes are what will make her family and friends love her. It is this obsession with having blue eyes along with being on the lower rung of the racial hierarchy, her family's poverty, the lack of friends and her very low self-esteem that drive Pecola slowly but surely insane. She slips into a world of fantasy where she has bluer-than-blue eyes and is the prettiest girl in the world.

Morrison grew up in the 1940s. Obviously the conditions facing blacks as she describes them in her novel are credible and authoritative. *The Bluest Eye* not only explores the issues of race, beauty, poverty, discrimination, abandonment, but also acquaints one with the hardships suffered by African Americans in the 1940s. This novel spurs a great amount of introspection, which is crucial in order to come to terms with such disturbing themes as rape, domestic violence and abject poverty. It incites feelings of disgust, anguish, anger and desperation. Morrison has not only written a novel with an achingly beautiful story but also created a series of painfully accurate impressions.

I am cut! And You ugly! (61)

The damage done was total. She spent her days, her tendril, sap-green days, walking up and down, up and down, her head jerking to the beat of a drummer so distant only she could hear. Elbows bent hands on the shoulders she flailed her arms like a bird in an eternal, grotesquely futile effort to fly. Beat the air, a winged but grounded bird, intent on the blue void it could not reach—could not even see—but which filled the valleys of the mind. (158)

The Black Fictional Heritage: The Place of Toni Morrison

> The ability of writers to imagine what is not the self, to familiarize the strange and mystify the familiar, is the test of their power.
>
> Toni Morrison

Toni Morrison, the eminent living writer, is the first African American woman to be awarded the Nobel Prize for Literature in 1993. Morrison's creative power often called 'Black Magic' encompasses within its folds mysticism, black folklore and mythology. Moreover, her fiction has been regarded as enigmatic, unconventional, and at times vague by her friends and foes in the same way. In her novels, trees talk, ghosts haunt houses, and people create holidays like National Suicide Day. Yet Morrison's spellbinding prose lures you in, locks the doors and encloses you in a special, very particular universe. (Strouse 52) There is no denying the fact that readers all over the world have acknowledged Morrison's genius unanimously. Morrison's voice has been a powerful one in literature because of her assessment of black experience, particularly black female experience within the fabric of black community.

Morrison was born Chloe Anthony Wofford, in the steel working town of Lorain, Ohio, in 1931. She grew up during the Great Depression of the 1930s in a poor but a very close-knit family. Morrison's mother, Rahmah Willis Wofford was from Alabama and George Wofford, her father came from Georgia. They were part of the Great Migration which was a large-scale movement of blacks from the rural agricultural South to the industrial cities of the North about 1880 to 1920. Both her parents' families moved to Ohio from the South to escape racism and to find better economic opportunities in the North. George Wofford, a ship welder hated and distrusted whites all his life. By her own admission her father was a racist. "As a child in Georgia, he received shocking impressions of adult white people, and for the rest of his life felt he was justified in despising all whites, and that they were not justified in despising him" (Strouse 52). On the other hand, her mother was a very religious woman who sang in the choir. She was an integrationist who unwaveringly believed that racial relations would improve with the economy. Though her parents held opposing views on race yet instilled in their children a conviction in the value of building self-reliance and looking up to the community as a means of support and aid during hard times. How crucial her family connection was could be measured from the fact that when she won the Nobel Prize she openly thanked God that her mother was still alive to see the extraordinary day of her life. Morrison's sense of who she is reveals the centrality of family heritage. The delineation of strong women and the relationships between three generations of women in a family in her novels strongly point to the time and influence of Morrison's mother, grandmother and her great grand mother on her. "The very black great grandmother with her white hair was the most powerful presence in Toni's childhood" (Russell 45).

The suasive factor paramount to Morrison's creativity was her family's legacy of the tradition of storytelling. Morrison maintained that a very important education was provided to her in her childhood through storytelling which was "a shared activity between the men and women of her family and that people of both gender participated in it . . . the children, were encouraged to participate in it at a very early age" (McKay 140-41). Even the folklore in her novels owe to this storytelling tradition. She regarded her father to be the best storyteller who narrated the scariest possible ghost stories. She was so fascinated by these stories that she made use of them in the manner she had heard them which gave her creative writing 'certain' authenticity.

Morrison began her own family in 1958. At Harvard, she fell in love with Harold Morrison who was a Jamaican architect. She had two sons from him. Unfortunately her marriage ended in divorce as she did not want to be subservient to him. She returned to her parents' house in Lorain with her two sons. She remained a single parent all along. To support herself and her children, Morrison took up a job as Associate Editor for a publishing company, Random House in Syracuse, New York. While editing books written by prominent black Americans like Muhammad Ali, Andrew Young and Angela Davis, she got an opportunity to dust off her own stories earlier written and translate them into novels. Her novels are like the beaded pearls where the thread runs through all the novels; each is a part of a whole. One work picks up where the other one leaves off either thematically or structurally or both. There is a strong sense of continuity in her novels. Each novel lays bare her acute insight into the psychological intent, predominantly that of the women and blacks in particular and of the human being in general. Her purpose as a writer is to present black life not simply as a study of a particular human group but in the full range of its profundity, gravity and generosity. She does not believe in sugarcoating the truth yet she does not base her characters on actual people as she thinks this makes the author a literary parasite who feeds on other person's lives to nourish her stories. Although each work is located within the black ghetto and focuses almost entirely on blacks within the larger white society, her novels have a universal appeal.

The central concern then of Morrison's novels is the black experience. Her creativity is intimately linked with her black experience and illustrates her deep interest in black people, their lives, culture, music, racial and social injustice and poverty faced by them. Her novels are not only creatively beautiful, they are also interrogations into the enigma of human behaviour. It is important to understand that her novels' unusual events which are at times disturbing connect to her self-characterization as a black woman novelist. Known for her candid portrayals of blacks, all her novels deal with individual pain and triumph of black characters where they struggle to find a foothold for themselves in an unwarranted unjust society. Her stories are all imaginative prose narratives, but nowhere can one find greater truths about life. The novels which are 'unquestionably and irrevocably' fantastic are an obvious means of expressing thoughts and processes that connect the present with the past. She explores the black experience from its roots in slavery to its vital presence in contemporary life.

A master storyteller, she tantalizes with pieces of information that are revealed in unhurried and meticulous ways, drawing one increasingly into the fascinating portrayals of events which alter lives forever. Her work presents issue of race, gender and class, with a familiarity that is poignant and often devastating. Her novels reflect her version of that experience that was excluded from both black male and white female writings. She strives to present the black women's quest for total freedom and takes us through many a chapter in black woman's life in the United States and see her grow from submissiveness to consciousness.

The words 'black' and 'women' have always been a dominant facet of her novel-writing and her persona. She insists on being known as a black woman novelist since black women write differently from white women, also because as a black and a woman she has a way of thinking and perceptions of a particular domain which is unavailable to people who were neither. She ostentatiously declares herself to be a black woman writer saying, "I get unnerved by all of it. When they say I'm a great American novelist, I say . . . 'they are trying to say I am not black'. When they say, I am a wonderful woman novelist . . . they think . . . I don't belong.' So I have just insisted . . . upon being called a black woman novelist." (Caldwell 243). She shares the spirit and solidarity of sisterhood as a typical black woman with other black women writers. "I write for black women. We are not addressing the men, as some white female writers do. We are not attacking each other as both black men and white men do" (Russell 46). Black women writers, she claims focus primarily on black men and women.

This is the most marked difference of all those combinations of black and white, male and female. "It's not so much that women write differently from men, but that black women write differently from white women. Black men don't write very differently from white men" (Tate 122). White male writers tend to be interested in writing about white men and white female writers contribute to this interest. Perhaps more amazingly is the fact that black male writers too are no different. They measure their identities and their power against those of their white male characters.

A writer par excellence, Morrison says, "Writing was for me the most extraordinary way of thinking and feeling. It became the one thing that I was doing that I had absolutely no intention of living without" (Watkins 45). As a writer she is frank and feisty because "it allows [me] to stretch and grow deeper I always wanted to, have some teeth in my work" (Micucii 278). For Morrison, writing is discovery and "talking deep within yourself, 'deep talking' as you say." (Tate 130).

She has always maintained that she writes for her people and candidly proclaimed, "I write . . . for *my* people" (LeClair 120), "I'm interested in black readers and me" (Brown 457). Focusing clearly on the blacks, she argues "If I could understand . . . then I assumed . . . that white people, if it was any good, would understand it also" (Bakerman 38). Morrison abhors the tone of apology in the black writings because as she puts it: "If I could understand Emily Dickinson—she wasn't writing for a Black audience or a White audience. She was writing whatever she wrote! I think if you do that, if you hone it on what you write, it will be universal . . . not the other way round" (Bakerman 38-39).

In Morrison's novels, women have been the story-tellers and bearer of history, as well as the instructor knowing the language of the blacks. Morrison is not a feminist in the typical sense of the word and it does not manifest itself blatantly. Her feminist concerns are obvious when she says that a woman can single-handedly run a house and that it is a very patriarchal notion that the head of a family has to be a male. She uses a beautiful metaphor to emphasize the fact that black women are much more suited to aggressiveness in the style recommended by archetype feminists. Black women have always been, she notes, "both safe harbor and ship" (Lester 48-49). Women have long held the dual responsibilities. They are the 'safe harbour' as they are endowed with the quality of nurturing and provide for financially as they are obviously the 'ship' anchoring to the safe harbour. She puts herself as an example of this as she raised her two sons single-handedly and proved that a woman is competent even without her male partner. She believes that women have a special kind of knowledge and when they get together they do not gossip but share information. She is more concerned with celebrating the unique feminine ethics that black women have developed in spite of their oppression. The feminist qualities that she advocates are traditional beauty, strength, resistance and integrity of black women. She is sensitive to feminist concerns and includes all these elements of black female experiences in her writing which are crucial to a woman. Morrison exposes the damages that sexist oppression, both inter and intra community have had on black women, but she does not allow these negative factors to characterise the whole of their experience. For Morrison feminism encourages allegiance to rather than an alienation from society. At the same time the existing hostility towards men bothers her. It is not as though men are above criticism but autonomy at the cost of somebody else being on his knee is deplorable.

One of the significant propagations of Morrison's Nobel lecture was her fundamental concern with language. The lecture can very well be called a eulogy to language as it is a building block of narrative with which a writer weaves together the past, present and future experiences of life. It is an instrument of power, which makes authority possible. Morrison, known for her rich poetic prose, blends in the images with a particular tempo of black speech and music to create a discourse of its own. The style is so deliciously poetic that it has to be leisurely savoured, nuances perceived, images cherished. Nobody can help but draw intellectual nourishment from her lyrical writing. Morrison weaves stories which connect epochs and generations knowing the power of words and that it can be used to make or mar humanity. In her hands, the language creates an extraordinary narrative of her people. There is a close link between Morrison's thematic concern and her use of language. She points out how the white writers had used language to erase the presence of blacks in their literature.

The most striking quality about her writing is specifically the black language of her people that she uses like "the saying of words, holding them on the tongue, experimenting with them, playing with them." (Le Clair 27) In a 1977 interview, she said that black people's charm has been what they do with language. The brutal life of the black is investigated with the lushness and vitality of her language as it does not develop in isolation. Man, milieu and memory create and nurture language. Part of her charisma lies in her extraordinary ability to create beautiful language, its oral quality, its ability to draw the reader in and to establish a participatory relationship with him or her.

Morrison desires to bring back the language that black people spoke, its original meanings, not the one sabotaged by constant abuse because of the slur of racism. She is very confident that "If you work very carefully, you can clean up ordinary words, and polish them, make parabolic language seem live again." (Tate 126) Morrison wants her language to provide primary means of sustaining a unique culture like music did for black people. Morrison deliberately accompanies her narrative with what might be called a sound track of black music. So we find her characters often break into folk songs, gospel numbers, popular tunes, the blues, or they simply whistle or hum when faced with intense happiness or pain.

Because language instead of becoming meaningful and therapeutic has been shackled and censored and spinned towards itself rather than become a place for human potential, Morrison has tried to break down the wall of silence in language. This is something of which she has spoken very eloquently. She passionately articulates the dangers that a maimed and mutilated language creates. Oppressive language represents violence, and obstruction of knowledge whether it is the ambiguous state language or the faux-language of senseless media; whether it is the proud but calcified language of academy or the commodity driven language of science; whether it is the malign language of the law without moral values, or language designed for the rupture of minorities, hiding its racist plunder in its fictional work—it must be discarded, changed and stripped.

Morrison endows her dialogues with "certain sound" (McKay 152) so that the story of black people (who could not write for themselves) could be told. Therefore we have the intentional oral quality in her works. She defends black people's language and counters the charges that black people speak in non-standard English. People fail to understand that it is basically a matter of handling of metaphor than the erroneous use of language. Morrison uses language to explore the ethnic mores of her people because it is the indispensable connection of knowledge bridging persons to their generation. Language ought to be a device for grappling with meaning, providing guidance and expressing love. As Morrison has often stated, one of her major tasks as a writer is "to clear the language up and give words back their original meaning, not the one that is sabotaged by constant use." (Tate 165)

Morrison is a colossal figure in the literary world, whose influence is felt among critics, scholars and authors alike. Her influence, like her writings, transcends race. She opened the channel to black experience, however disquieting, for everyone. Morrison has in each of her novels dared herself to explore the power and sense of self that can emerge directly from confronting one's societal and personal histories. She like any marginalized writer has journeyed through the various stages in her creative writing—an initial stage of anger, then self-discovery, which leads to a period during which the writer celebrates her culture, before arriving at a complex understanding of the ethnic experience. Her intricate and meticulously detailed novels persistently haunt and move people. The precise language and potent mystery compels careful reading and re-reading. In addition to being one of the United States's most celebrated black writers, she is undeniably the most compelling female voice. Morrison focuses extensively on the issues such as racism and love within the framework of everyday relationship and provides insight into both love and hatred that exist in the human psyche.

The Novels

Critical recognition and praise for Morrison grew with each novel. Morrison has written eight novels—from *The Bluest Eye* in 1970 through *Love* in 2003. Her first six major novels—*The Bluest Eye*, *Song of Solomon*, *Sula*, *Tar Baby*, *Beloved*, and *Jazz*—have collected nearly every major literary prize. *Paradise* was written after the Nobel Prize followed by *Love*.

The Bluest Eye (1970) recounts the saga of a young black girl Pecola Breedlove, a victim of rape by her father. She thinks that all her problems would vanish if only she had blue eyes. She considers herself ugly, a fact which is unfortunately reiterated by everyone she meets in her young life. In order to conform to the ideal of white beauty, Pecola despises her blackness which leads to the spiralling down of her self-esteem resulting in her madness. All the characters in the novel make every effort "to get rid of the funkiness" (68) by repressing their black characteristics which are not suited to white feminity. Pecola fails to understand that it is not what you look like that matters but who you are!

Sula (1973) is the story of a stormy friendship between Sula Peace and Nel Wright, who are diametrically opposite by way of connecting to other people, to the world around them, and to their own self. In fact, they are the two faces of the same coin. By providing a contrast with Nel, Morrison brings out the predominant qualities of Sula's persona. What is interesting is that Morrison portrays the two girls in terms of negatives, i.e. what they are not rather than what they are. She uses these negatives to highlight the utter lack of form. Each girl gains from the other that has been blatantly denied to them in their homes—protection, loving care, integrity and coherence. The differences in their personalities complement one another in a way that forges an almost unbreakable alliance. Like Pecola, Sula is the scapegoat of the black community and is treated like a pariah. If Pecola's lunacy begets sanity in people, then Sula's evil sinfulness make other people feel righteous.

Morrison's third novel, *Song of Solomon* (1977), is a rhapsodic epic where a man's determination to fly takes him home again. Milkman Dead is born under the influence of "flying." His flying is not just literal—it is a metaphor for his identity quest—flying towards his ancestral and cultural roots. Milkman's efforts to trace his roots leads him to discover his 'ancient properties' and he realizes that he cannot fly without embracing his past as the air underneath his wings. He learns if one attempts to fly solo without human connections, without knowledge of the past, and without true love, then not only is that one capable of killing others but also one's identity and culture. The final image of flight lacks a definitive conclusion and Milkman's fate is very ambiguous. However, the issue is not whether he lives or dies, but whether he finds his roots or gets his wings clipped.

Tar Baby (1981), Morrison's fourth novel, is the story of a tumultuous romance between a gorgeous black supermodel, and an earthy sensual black man who is everything she both dreads and desires. The only thing that is common between the two is the colour of their skin. Jadine is a cultural orphan because she finds herself torn between the black world and the white world, fitting into neither. Son, the intruder in more ways than one, never really finds a place in society for himself because of what he represents. Morrison contrasts the Eurocentric culture where Jadine is the white woman in black skin against a mythical blackness, represented by Son with his "elemental rawness." *Tar Baby* not only explores the relationship between a man and a woman but also between black and white, black and black, parent and child, urban and rural issues.

The Pulitzer winning *Beloved* (1987) is an absorbing tale based on a true story of the life of Margaret Garner, an escaped black slave who killed her child to prevent it from being taken back into slavery. *Beloved* is as much about the mother-daughter bonding as it is about the crimes of bondage (slavery). Sethe in an ultimate gesture of a "mother love" chooses to kill her baby girl rather than allowing her to be exposed to the physical and emotional damages wrecked by slavery. Sethe is as much haunted by Beloved's presence as she was by her absence because any kind of hold involving human beings is destructive. Morrison uses historical fact to depict the brutalities and barbarism committed in the name of slavery. *Beloved* is not simply a story of Sethe who survive and escape slavery, but it is the saga of people like her who were haunted by slavery's legacy. The novel looks on three generations of women—Baby Suggs, who was born in Africa and brought to America as a slave, Sethe her daughter-in-law who suffered unbearably as a slave and Denver, her granddaughter who represents hope for the future generations of black women. *Beloved* is an intriguing tale which informs that it is not an experience but a story to pass on.

*Jazz (*1992), the sixth novel, is a story of a love triangle between a man, his wife and his teenage lover. It portrays the monstrous potential of love and the ensuing moral ambiguity. The living memory of Joe Trace's dead lover, Dorcas becomes a disturbing presence in his and wife Violet Trace's lives, bringing back past reminiscences along with unsettled and agonizing issues to the fore. In *Jazz,* Morrison manages to accomplish a literary feat capturing the very essence and character of a genre of music and translating it into literature. So like the music of jazz the novel is seductive yet sad, lively yet unpretentious, and is simultaneously a fête of and tirade against life. Morrison does not attempt to offer a rational explanation of the seemingly bizarre behavior of the main characters; instead she delves deep into the human consciousness, into the very core of events which shape and at times warp the human mind.

Paradise (1998) is a colossal work where Morrison holds up a mirror and dares all blacks to look in. It is a harrowing tale of a small group of people bent on ethical cleansing of their township. They take upon themselves to create their own paradise on earth. It is a paradise torn apart by murder and mayhem. This group of blacks establishes their own impenetrable community since they think of themselves as racially authentic and original descendents of Africa; looking down on whites and even blacks of lower origin. They think that the evil in their town is due to the presence of the strange women who live in a Convent seventeen miles outside of Ruby. A deadly confrontation breaks out as these blacks go on a lethal chase to annihilate the four women and a baby of the Convent. It's a tale of paradise lost. It is also a story of displacement and exodus; of the dangers of racial intolerance and misplaced chauvinism; of escapism and refuge; of people looking for communal approval and non-judgmental support. Morrison makes use of both Ruby and the Convent, to assess critically the utopian ideal as ridiculous, hazardous and deceptive. It is the mind which makes a heaven of hell and hell of heaven.

Love (2003) is a telling novel that explores several unexpected aspects of one of the potent human emotions ever experienced. It is a tale of warped love between two women—Heed and Christine and how it affects their lives. The powerful spectre of Bill Cosey—a rich black hotel owner—is the catalyst to the story. Once upon a time these girls were childhood friends until Bill Cosey, Christine's grandfather, married Heed when she was only 11 years old and he 52. He hopes that Heed, the *virgo Intacta* will bear him a son to replace the one he lost to death. From that point onwards the bitterness between the two grew and continued over the next 2-3 decades. They exude a palpable hatred for one another and wait for the other to die which would make the other entitled to Cosey's will to gain his entire estate. The novel deals with the intrigues of love lost, found and given away, walled by insanity, self-indulgence and hatred. If *Beloved* explores parental love, *Jazz* a romantic love and *Paradise* a religious love, then *Love* explores covetous love.

Works Cited

Bakerman, Jane. "The Seams Can't Show: An Interview with Toni Morrison," *Conversations with Toni Morrison*, ed. Danille Taylor-Guthrie, Jackson: UP of Mississippi, 1994. 30-42.

Brown, Cecil. "Interview with Toni Morrison," *Massachusetts Review*. 36.3, 1995.

Caldwell, Gail. "Author Toni Morrison Discusses Her Latest Novel *Beloved*," *Conversations with Toni Morrison*, ed. Danille Taylor-Guthrie. 239-45.

LeClair, Thomas. "The Language Must Not Sweat: A Conversation with Toni Morrison," *Conversations with Toni Morrison*, ed. Danille Taylor-Guthrie.119-28.

Lester, Rosemarie K. "An Interview with Toni Morrison." Hessian Radio Network, Frankfurt, West Germany," *Critical Essays on Toni Morrison*, ed. Nellie McKay, Boston: G.K. Hall, 1988.

McKay, Nellie. "An Interview with Toni Morrison," *Conversations with Toni Morrison*, ed. Danille Taylor-Guthrie. 138-55.

Micucci, Dana. "An Inspired Life: Toni Morrison Writes and a Generation Listens." *Conversations with Toni Morrison*, ed. Danille Taylor-Guthrie. 275-79.

Russell, Sandi. "It's OK to say OK," *Critical Essays on Toni Morrison*, ed. Nellie McKay. 43-47.

Strouse, Jean. "Toni Morrison: Black Magic," *Newsweek*. 30 March, 1981.

Tate, Claudia, ed. "Toni Morrison," *Black Women Writers at Work*. New York: Continuum, 1983. 117-31.

Watkins, Mel. "Talk with Toni Morrison," *Conversations with Toni Morrison*, ed. Danille Taylor-Guthrie. 43-47.

The Bluest Eye: A Detailed Analysis

The events in *The Bluest Eye* are not presented chronologically, neither are the chapters marked. For the convenience of the readers, the chapters have been numbered.

Foreword I

The story of *The Bluest Eye* is set in motion with two untitled forewords of one-page each.

The novel commences with a 1940s first grade children's Primer:

- Here is the house. It is green and white. It has a red door. It is very pretty. Here is the family. Mother, Father, Dick and Jane live in the green-and-white house. They are very happy.
- Here is the house it is green and white it has a red door it is very pretty here is the family mother father dick and jane live in the green-and-white house they are very happy
- Hereisthehouseitisgreenandwhiteithasareddooritisverypretty hereisthefamilymotherfatherdickandjaneliveinthegreenandw hitehousetheyareveryhappy

The excerpt from *Dick and Jane* demonstrates how the socio-cultural influences shape and mould the thinking and perception of people. The neatly secure and comfortable family life depicted in the primer is a far cry from the poverty ridden, uncertain, and ravaged lives of the black families. The family circle complete with cat and dog is drawn from the Western culture matrix. Morrison builds the novel on the almost unspeakable contrasts of the excerpt's utopian land where white children live a blissful life with their parents in a perfect house with a white picket fence and pets and friends whereas for the Breedloves, home is horrible if it can be called home at all. It is a place where parents engage in physical scuffle and intentionally harm and abuse their children.

The excerpt is repeated three times. It starts to become compressed and incomprehensible. The first time the story is written clearly. The second time however, this sequence is repeated verbatim without punctuation, and then, it is repeated a third time without spaces between the words or punctuation. The remarkable, reassuring rhythm undergoes a nightmarish acceleration, and the sentences run together without breaks.

The first version illustrates just how threatening this idealized representation could be in small town vicinity and what can happen to a black child who cannot stop judging herself against the standards of whiteness. This apparently straightforward idea of perfection is so distant from the lives of the Breedloves that although they are expected to value it, they have no means of attaining it. This preliminary part foreshadows the major events of the plot.

Foreword II

The second account is a one page italicized preface narrated by Claudia MacTeer as an adult. She speaks in a very warm trusting manner while she takes readers into her confidence. Claudia narrates what happened in the fall of the year 1941 in Lorain, Ohio. The marigolds in their garden and around did not bloom. She says that she and her sister Frieda thought that the marigolds did not bloom because Pecola Breedlove was having her father's baby. For years Claudia thought that Frieda was right in blaming her for she had planted the seeds too deep inside the earth. But now, she wonders that perhaps the earth itself was barren. Claudia connects the earth to Pecola and equates the planting of marigold seeds in the black dirt to Pecola's father "dropping his seeds in his own plot of black dirt" (9). Looking back Claudia realizes nothing came off their fears and expectations. Neither the flowers bloomed nor did the baby live. She goes on to explain that Cholly died and so did Claudia's innocence.

The words "quiet as it's kept" (9) highlights the fact that the story is unusual but imperative enough for Claudia to narrate and that the phrase was a familiar way of black women gossiping and sharing secrets with one another and children eavesdropping on them. Therefore the story comes through a child's perspective.

The second description specifies the source of Pecola's tragedy: "There is really nothing more to say except why. But since *why* is difficult to handled, one must take refuge in *how*." (9) One will never know why the incest occurred, however the novel attempts to ask "how," examining Pecola's life and the impact of social constructions and the forces responsible for her tragedy.

Chapter I: AUTUMN: Nuns go by as quiet as lust . . .

This is the first of the four main sections of the novel. It is the autumn of 1940. It is a time when America is still reeling under the impact of the Great Depression. Claudia MacTeer's family, though much better off than the other blacks, is struggling through hard times. Claudia narrates the first part of the story. She is nine years old and lives in an old ramshackle house. Their house is infested with cockroaches and rodents. They have a single kerosene lamp while rest of the house is dark. Their cold green house is antithetical to the white picket fence house of Dick and Jane. As children, they are to be seen and not heard. The adults in their lives "do not talk [to us]—they give [us] directions." (12) Claudia and Frieda eavesdrop on gossips about people while doing dishes. This is how Claudia comes to know all the scandal.

Claudia remembers her early days of poverty. She talks about her life and her surroundings. She and Frieda live next door to Rosemary Villanucci who is a white girl. They crave what Rosemary's white privilege bestows on her i.e. good food, ownership and benefits. With the start of school, Claudia and Frieda are taken to the railway tracks where they gather coal that has fallen out of the trains. During one such trip, Claudia catches a cold. Her mother nurses her through illness with constant nagging and complaining. However, despite her mother's anger, Claudia realizes that her mother conceals enormous love and concern for her daughter and that she is really angry at the illness itself. Claudia's house has something which makes it different from others and that is the covert and constant love of their mother.

That autumn, the MacTeers accepted two new people—Mr. Henry Washington, who was a rent-paying boarder, and Pecola Breedlove, who had been temporarily taken into custody by the state—into their family. When Henry Washington arrived, Claudia and her sister were not introduced to him but "merely pointed out" (16), along with other household furniture and rest of the rooms. When Henry spoke to them, they were astonished. They found him wonderful and liked him since he played with them, and entertained them with magic tricks. They were fascinated with him as he compared them to the white Hollywood actresses Greta Garbo and Ginger Rogers. However the narrative of Mr. Henry's arrival ends on a gloomy note with Claudia saying: "Even after what came later, there was no bitterness in our memory of him." (16)

The second addition, Pecola Breedlove, comes to stay with Claudia's family for a few days because her drunkard father, Cholly Breedlove, has burnt down the house that the Breedloves lived in. Cholly is sent to jail while Pecola's brother Sammy moves in with another family, and her mother Pauline stays with the white family for whom she works. The black community called Cholly the "old Dog Breedlove," (17) as he stooped to the level of an animal by putting his family "outdoors" (17). Claudia describes Pecola's situation as pathetic since she understands how terrible it is to lose one's house in such difficult times. As the blacks are forced to live a peripheral existence, the prospect of 'being put outdoors' has a serious connotation. By the community standards, being put outdoors is the worst condition that could happen to a person; therefore everybody feels awful for Pecola and regards her with pity.

Claudia remembers the days when Pecola came to stay with them. Claudia and Frieda were thrilled to have a friend. They stopped fighting with each other and treated Pecola as a guest in their house. Pecola, a year older than Frieda, was a timid shy girl; less mature than the two MacTeer sisters. She had come to the MacTeers with nothing; not even a set of undergarments. She appreciates the kindheartedness shown by Claudia and Frieda.

Pecola loves drinking milk out of the blue and white Shirley Temple cup the girls bring her. She is mesmerized by the blue-eyed, golden-haired, dimple-faced Shirley Temple. She and Frieda talk about the beauty of Shirley Temple. Mrs. MacTeer is annoyed because Pecola begins drinking a lot of milk (three quarts) out of that cup just to gaze adoringly at the Shirley Temple picture.

On the other hand, Claudia hates Shirley Temple. In fact, she hates all things white, blond haired and blue eyed—including dolls, movie stars, and even little white girls like Rosemary Villanucci. She remembers an incident from her childhood when she had received a blue-eyed white-faced doll for Christmas that she destroyed by dismembering it. Instead of adoring the doll, like most other children would do, Claudia loathed it. She tears apart the doll to find out where lies its "beauty" because "Adults, older girls, shops, magazines, newspapers, window sign—all the world had agreed that a blue-eyed, yellow-haired, pink-skinned doll was what every girl child treasured" (20-21) She concedes that it was wrong on her part to behave in such an aggressive manner but she wanted to discover what made black women appreciate white beauty and what eluded her. She furthermore does not like Shirley Temple because she has seen her dancing with Bojangles in one of the movies. Claudia considers Bojangles to be her uncle, her pal, and thinks that he should be dancing with her, not the white girl.

Claudia also remembers the day she witnessed the onset of Pecola's first period. Having been forced by Mrs. MacTeer's bad temper, the three girls are sitting outside on the steps when Pecola becomes conscious that she is bleeding between her legs. The initial reactions of the three girls range from ignorance to terror to wonder. Frieda understands that Pecola is "ministratin" (25) and decides to try and take care of the problem herself. She asks Claudia to get some water to wash off the steps while she tries to attach a pad to Pecola's dress. Unfortunately for the girls,

Rosemary, who has been watching from the bushes, tells Mrs. MacTeer that the girls are "playing nasty." (27) Before the girls can explain what has happened, Mrs. MacTeer starts to thrash Frieda hard. It is only when she sees the pad coming undone that she realizes what had happened and cleans up Pecola. Claudia looks at the new and different Pecola with awe and reverence.

That night while going to bed, Pecola asks Frieda if it is true that now she can have a baby. Frieda answers in affirmation saying that one has to find "somebody . . . to love [you]." (29) Pecola is not concerned with her new physical ability to bear children; instead the idea of someone loving her overwhelms her as she has never felt loved by anyone. She asks a very simple yet ironical question "How do you get someone to love you?" (29) The girls have no answer to this. The chapter ends poignantly with Pecola wondering how she will ever find someone to love her.

Chapter II: HEREISTHEHOUSE . . .

This short chapter begins with the history of the house in which the Breedloves live. The tiny store-front apartment where Pecola and her family live stands in startling contrast to the ideal green and white house of the primer. It is a bleak, colorless, abandoned storefront building neither rich nor interesting as Dick and Jane's house is a pretty green and white house. Pecola's house is anything but that!

The narrator describes the derelict and dilapidated store that sits "on the southeast corner of Broadway and Thirty-Fifth Street in Lorain, Ohio." (30) Before it was abandoned, it used to be a storefront. It passed through many hands. It was once a pizza parlour and a favourite hangout for teenage boys. Prior to that, the place was let out to a Hungarian baker. Much before that, it was a real-estate office and even earlier a Gypsy family lived here. The place was filled with life and spirit. The Breedloves were the last residents. They live in the storefront because they are poor and black.

Now the house is a cause of sore eyes to anyone passing by who cannot but wonder as to why the building was not pulled down. The local community, on the other hand, ignores the very presence of the Breedlove house. Although there is no life left in the house nevertheless it gives the Breedlove a sense of belonging and ownership. It is divided into two rooms by a flimsy wall of wooden planks. The front room has two sofas, a piano, and a grimy artificial Christmas tree not cared for. There is a bedroom where all the Breedloves sleep. There are three beds, one for Pecola, another for her older brother, Sammy, and a double bed for Cholly and Pauline. An unreliable coal stove sits in the centre of the room for heat. The kitchen is a separate room at back. There is no bathing facility, only a toilet bowl placed not very discreetly.

Chapter III: HEREISTHEFAMILY . . .

This chapter, like the previous one, begins with a short, unpunctuated, excerpt from the Dick and Jane primer ironically cut short before the word 'happy.' It talks about the ultimate white family consisting of Mother, Father, Dick, and Jane, all of whom live in the very pretty green and white house. The narrator subsequently introduces the Breedlove family who are antithetical to the white family of the primer—poor, black, wretched, and convinced of their ugliness. The Breedloves are ruinously influenced by what others think of them. Their ugliness comes not so much from their actual physical appearance as from their belief that they are ugly. It was not their poverty which was unique but their ugliness because poverty was "traditional and stultifying." (34) They are ugly because they believe they are ugly. Others think they are poor and ugly, and so they think of themselves as poor and ugly, and do not strive for more.

Cholly and Pauline are locked into a violent marriage, even as Pecola and Sammy brace themselves to suffer their parents' fierce fighting.

The story that currently unfolds takes place on a Saturday morning in October. The previous evening Cholly had come home drunk. Mrs. Breedlove gets up in the morning, and goes to the kitchen. She is angry with Cholly and demands that he goes outside and get some coal for her. Cholly refuses. She threatens that if she sneezes just once from bringing coal for the stove from outside, he is in trouble. It is clear that a physical fight between them is going to ensue because each of Cholly's drunken incidents ends in a fight with his wife. The narrator reveals that these awful fights which are brutal though not long drawn, have a ritualistic pattern and are "calculated, uninspired, and deadly." (35) Mrs. Breedlove throws a pot of cold water over Cholly. He in turn knocks her down. She strikes him with the pot and he hits her in the face. Sammy joins in and beats up his father with his fists calling him names. Mrs. Breedlove strikes Cholly with a stove top, knocking him unconscious and goes about her housekeeping.

The children deal with the fighting in different ways. Though this is a regular feature in the Breedlove house, it is undeniably very painful to Pecola. Every time this happens she prays to God to make her disappear, so that she would no longer have to deal with the problems at home. Sammy on the other hand frequently runs away. Pecola very much wants her brother to take her along with him when he runs away. With a child's logic she imagines that if she weren't so ugly Sammy would have taken her along.

Pecola lived an unblessed life. She loathes herself and wonders what is it about her that makes her teachers ignore her, classmates spurn her and parents neglect her. Pecola dreams of blue eyes, a present that she thinks will at once change her into a thing of beauty. The narrator describes her longing thus "Long hours she sat looking in the mirror, trying to discover the secret of the ugliness, the ugliness that made her ignored or despised at school, by teachers and classmates alike." (39) She believes that if she were beautiful, and had blue eyes, then the darkness of her abysmal world would be removed, she would have friends to play with, and her own parents would stop quarrelling and start loving her. So Pecola fervently prays for blue eyes, trusting that if she were pretty, ugly things wouldn't happen.

The narrative switches to present tense. Pecola walks down Garden Avenue to Mr. Yacobowski's grocery store. On her way she recognises the familiar and cherished images of her world, particularly the dandelions at the base of the telephone pole. She finds them beautiful and cannot understand why people consider them ugly and think of them simply as weeds. She has three pennies with her and decides to buy Mary Jane candies for herself. Mr. Yacobowski looks over the counter at her but looks right through her. He does not understand what she is pointing at. She has trouble communicating with him because when she looks up at him she sees "the total absence of human recognition—the glazed separateness." (42) The racialized gaze paralyzes her response because of which she is unable to voice her desire. This in turn reinforces his contempt for her. He has very little patience and definitely no love for her. Ultimately she succeeds in buying three Mary Jane candies. When she reaches out to hand him the money, he hesitates for a moment as he does not want to touch her hand. She understands that Mr. Yacobowski needs to take the money so he extends his hands, just like people who take the leaves of the dandelions for making soup and wine, but no one wants the head of it. She realizes that she is like the dandelion no one wants in their yard. The dandelions which she considered beautiful sometime earlier are no more the same.

Her humiliation at the hands of Yacobowski strengthens the old idea that ugliness is inherent and cannot be changed by a different way of perceiving the world. She too agrees like everyone else that the dandelions are in fact unsightly. Walking back home, Pecola is initially angry but later filled with shame. She concludes that dandelions are ugly, whereas Mary Jane picture on the candy wrapper is gorgeous. Each wrapper has a picture of a smiling white girl with blond hair and blue eyes. Pecola slowly unwraps her candy and admires the picture of blonde, blue-eyed Mary Jane. She has what Pecola desires. Pecola thinks that if she eats the candies, then she too will become like Mary Jane, so Pecola voraciously consumes Mary Jane candies constantly staring at the wrapper.

After the terrible domestic scene mentioned earlier, Pecola snuggles up to the three black prostitutes who live in the apartment above hers. China, Poland, and Miss Marie are good-natured and affectionate with her but are an inadequate substitute for the family Pecola is missing. Yet she enjoys talking to and being around with them. They let her call on them and run errands for them. They are neither women whose innocence has been corrupted nor prostitutes with hearts of gold. They experience no shame nor feel victimized by their profession and cheerfully and unsentimentally abhor men with a vengeance. There is no love lost between them and their community.

Pecola sits and talks with them wanting to know all about their lives and their 'boyfriends' (Pecola's term for their customers). Marie tells Pecola a story about how she turned one of her boyfriends over to the FBI and about the man she really loved Dewey Prince. Pecola starts to think about love. Her mind wonders to her parents' lovemaking and she becomes confused. She remembers her father making a lot of noise as though he is in great pain and her mother not making any noise as if she is suffocating or choking.

The chapter ends with Pecola turning from the window and looking at the three women intently. China is doing and re-doing her self. Poland is once again singing another Blues song about a soft-brown boy and Marie shells peanuts and eats them earnestly. Pecola speculates if they are for real.

Chapter IV: WINTER: My daddy's face is a study

In this chapter we are once again within Claudia's narrative which continues through the winter that "tightened our heads with a band of cold and melted our eyes." (52) Winter appears bringing in its wake boredom and a long wait for spring.

The chapter begins with Claudia eulogizing her father. She describes her father's face as being very cold and harsh like winter. Claudia speaks about the severity of winter and her father's resilience as he works night and day to keep the family safe and financially secure. His steely, intimidating eyes become a "cliff of snow threatening to avalanche," (52) and "his eyebrows bend like black limbs of leafless trees." (52) At a time when everyone in the house is squeezing themselves tight in the cold of winter he is the one who takes care of the heater; he is the one who educates his daughters on how to distinguish between which doors to open and which to close, how to gather, supply and store the fire. Mr. MacTeer is a stark contrast to the previous chapter's narrative of Cholly Breedlove. MacTeer, like his wife, is a no-nonsense, hard-working man who shows his love for his family more through his conduct than through his expressions.

The monotony of the winter is broken by Maureen Peal, a light-skinned, light-eyed, long-haired wealthy black girl who casts a spell of charm on the entire school. She is somewhat more "white" than other black people and Claudia and Frieda are jealous yet fascinated by her. Claudia frequently pictures hurting Maureen as she is held in high esteem by the teachers and other students. Claudia associates her with the white doll that was given to her one Christmas. She tries to strip Maureen of her influence by calling her namess. The two sisters soon find out that Maureen has a dog tooth and that she was born with an extra finger on each hand and still has little bumps where they used to be. They call her "Six-finger-dog-tooth-meringue-pie." (61)

One warm morning Maureen chooses to walk with Claudia and Frieda the way home. They come upon Pecola who is being harassed by a group of boys for her blackness and being tormented for her father's supposed habit of sleeping naked. They hurl choicest of insults by calling her, "Black e mo. Black e mo. Ya daddy sleep nekked." (*55*) Pecola is distraught and sobs uncontrollably. Frieda comes to her rescue and holds her hand and guides her away. Frieda hits one of the boys and threatens another. Claudia joins in. The two sisters stand up to the boys and force them to leave Pecola alone. Maureen also stands up for Pecola. It seems as though the boys will beat up the MacTeer sisters, but Maureen's arrival turns the events as the boys do not want to fight in front of Maureen. They go away pretending that they have no time for girls. The four girls begin to walk home. Maureen introduces herself to Pecola and asks if Pecola got her name from a movie called *Imitation of Life* where a mulatto girl hates her black mother but cries at her funeral. Pecola can only sigh. Claudia and Frieda are very happy to see Maureen being friendly to Pecola. The four girls stop at the Isaley's ice cream parlour which only Maureen can afford to have. She buys an ice cream for Pecola. Claudia and Frieda stare at it with greed but act as if they don't want any. At first Maureen talks about movies with Pecola. They pass a theatre with a picture of Betty Grable on it. Both Maureen and Pecola agree that Betty Grable is superb. On the other hand, Claudia thinks that Hedy Lamarr is more sophisticated.

The conversation turns to puberty and Maureen asks Pecola if she menstruates. She proudly declares she does. Then remembering the boys' conversation, Maureen inquires from Pecola if she has ever seen a naked man. The question clearly makes Pecola uncomfortable. For some reason she thinks that she is being asked if she has seen her father naked, which she passionately refutes even though she knows it is true. She tells Maureen that no father would be naked in front of his daughter because that would be shameful and indecent. Maureen presses on. Claudia and Frieda try to stop Maureen but in vain. Claudia thinks of the time when she and Frieda had seen their own father naked. She remembers the embarrassment and odd curiosity in seeing father naked.

The conversation rapidly turns into a quarrel. Maureen starts to taunt all the three girls. Claudia is happy to have an opportunity to show her resentment towards Maureen. She hits out on her but Maureen safely runs to the other side of the road. Claudia calls Maureen "dog tooth" and "boy-crazy" (60) and Maureen in turn jeers at them: "I am cute! And you ugly! Black and ugly black e mos. I am cute!" (61) This is disturbing for all the three girls but it is Pecola who is most affected. Claudia vividly narrates Pecola's condition who "seemed to fold into herself, like a pleated wing." (61) Though Claudia is visibly upset but she realizes that Maureen is not the real enemy. The real enemy is the "*Thing* that made her beautiful" (62) and them unattractive.

When Claudia and Frieda reach home, only Mr. Henry is there. The girls smell turnips being cooked and call out for their mother. Henry comes down wearing his bathrobe through which his hairless legs can be seen. He tells them that their mother is not at home and that she has instructions for them to turn down the stove and have some graham crackers. Henry gives them money to buy ice cream. The girls decide to buy candies as they do not want to run into Maureen once again in the ice cream parlour. Upon their sudden arrival, they see Henry amusing the prostitutes the Maginot Line and China in the living room. They find him licking one of the prostitute's fingers.

The girls are taken aback to see these prostitutes in their home, particularly Maginot Line, who is considered the most immoral woman to walk on the face of the earth (by the church women). After the prostitutes leave, Claudia and Frieda inquire about his female visitors. He tells them that the prostitutes are in fact members of his Bible study group. They feel let down when Henry lies to them but pretends to believe his ridiculous explanation. He tells them not to inform their mother and the girls decide to keep Henry's clandestine meeting with the whores a secret. The chapter ends with Claudia and Frieda cooking turnips and eating graham crackers, as they wait for their mother to come home.

Chapter V: SEETHECATGOESMEOW . . .

This chapter opens with an excerpt from the primer about the cat the two white children play with. It is a perfect playful cat living in a perfect white family. This is in stark contrast to cat depicted in the story that follows.

This section opens with a vivid passage recounting the places from where many young black women come from to Lorain. These women hail from the Southern rural towns like Mobile, Aiken, Newport News, Marietta, and Meridian. ". . . these girls soak up the juice of their home towns, and it never leaves them." (67) They are typical women who marry typical men and live in typical houses they call home. They are women who take special care of themselves and their clothing. They are the educated blacks who think of themselves as "colored people" and view themselves as superior to other blacks, whom they refer to as "niggers." These women struggle to get rid of the blackness concerning trying to look and act like white people—an attribute Morrison calls "funkiness." (68)

The narrative moves swiftly from the general to the specific, zeroing in on a woman called Geraldine. She lives with her husband Louis and a son named Louis Junior. Mother, Father, and son epitomize the black middle class, who have wandered off from their black roots. Junior grows up in an excessively hygienic, but emotionally oppressive surroundings. He does not receive any nurturing from either his parents and is not allowed to play with other black children. Geraldine also has a cat whom she loves more than her son. As the cat is a non-messy animal, she touches and hugs it the way she should be doing to her son.

Geraldine does everything in her power to separate herself from any thing black and is concerned only with things white. She is a complete autocrat who controls her home and her own body. Geraldine has told her son that there is a great difference between coloured people and niggers. She has explained it to him that as they belong to the first kind and therefore they have to maintain certain standards of behaviour more in line with white middleclass sensibilities. She makes it clear to him that coloured people are clean and sober whereas niggers are filthy and loud. He longs to play with the black kids of the block but he has to play with the "white kids; his mother did not like him to play with niggers. She had explained to him the difference between colored people and niggers. They were easily identifiable. Colored people were neat and quiet; niggers were dirty and loud." (71) She persuades Junior to play with white children and dresses him like the whites do.

Geraldine lives in a lovely house next to the Washington Irving School, which is attended by Pecola, Frieda and Claudia. Junior realizes early on that his mother likes the cat more than him and therefore he has intense hatred of the cat. He becomes malevolent toward the cat, tortures it and waits for an opportunity to kill it. As he is not allowed to play with black children, and white children do not play with him, Junior grows into a bully and vents his frustration by terrorizing other children coming to play in the nearby park.

One day when Pecola is walking alone through the playground, she becomes Junior's target as he decides to pick on her because he is fed up and lonely. He calls her over and promises to show her some kittens. Initially she refuses but Junior pleads with her to come in. Once inside Pecola is mesmerized by the beautiful interior of the house and its furniture. Junior chooses this moment to throw his mother's big black cat on Pecola's face. The cat scratches Pecola. She is terrified and tries to leave the house. Junior runs towards the door to prevent her from doing so. The cat starts to rub itself against Pecola's leg, and she is fascinated by the blue-eyed black cat. She begins to caress the cat. Seeing this, Junior grabs the cat by its leg and begins to swing it in circles.

Junior comes back in because he can no longer hear Pecola crying. He grabs the cat and swings it around. Pecola desperately tries to save the cat but in the struggle she falls on Junior, who lets go of the animal. The cat gets flung against the window and falls onto the radiator and collapses. Geraldine arrives home, and Junior holds Pecola responsible for the cat's death.

Geraldine is repulsed by Pecola's presence in her house as she represents everything that Geraldine loathes—dirty, matted hair, torn dress, black poverty, and black ugliness. Geraldine calls Pecola a "nasty little black bitch" (75) and orders her to get out of her house. Pecola is distraught and powerless. She quietly makes her way home in the snow. The last image that stays with Pecola while stumbling out is the "sad and unsurprised" (76) gaze of Christ to whom she prays to grant her blue eyes.

Chapter VI: SPRING: The first twigs are thin . . .

This section called 'Spring' is narrated by Claudia in first-person. Her memories of springs are associated with being spanked by forsythia twigs instead of a strap. These thrashings hurt them much more than being hit by a belt strap or even a hairbrush. She remembers that the forsythia twigs would bend with force but never break. Even today, she takes no delight in seeing the forsythia.

One spring day, Claudia comes home and finds Frieda crying. Claudia thinks that Frieda must have been spanked by her mother; instead Frieda breaks down and tells her that Henry had touched her breasts. When she tells her parents about the sexual assault, they badly beat Henry up. Her father even tried to shoot Henry but missed as he runs away down the road. Hearing the commotion, Rosemary Villanucci comes out and tells Frieda that her father would go to jail and so gets beaten up by Frieda. Miss Dunion, another neighbour, comes in and advises the MacTeers to take Frieda to the doctor for she might be "ruined." Frieda cannot stop crying because she is confused about what the word means. Since their mother has used it to describe the prostitutes, the two girls mistakenly assumed it means 'fat' and are concerned that Frieda will now become fat like the Maginot Line. Claudia consoles Frieda by telling her she could drink whiskey because their mother had told them that Poland and China were not fat as whiskey was eating them up.

In order to keep Frieda from getting overweight, Claudia and Frieda decide to ask Pecola for whiskey as her father is drunk all the time. They go to Pecola's house, but she is not at home. They find the Maginot Line drinking root beer who informs them that Pecola is helping her mother at her workplace. Her mother, Pauline, works for a white family named Fisher.

Pecola is pleased to see them. They talk about the Maginot Line. Meanwhile Mrs. Breedlove calls the girls inside and asks them to stay put while she goes downstairs to get the laundry. While she's gone, a white girl comes in with golden hair and fluffy bedroom slippers. She is frightened when she sees three black girls and asks where Polly is. Claudia considers this an insult because even Pecola who is Pauline's daughter calls her Mrs. Breedlove.

Frieda notices a bowl of freshly baked berry cobbler sitting by the stove. As the three girls move closer to inspect it, Pecola accidentally pulls it off the counter. It spills all over the floor scalding her little legs severely with hot liquid. When Pauline comes in, she lets loose a barrage of angry words upon her daughter. She seizes Pecola and bangs her to the floor and beats her. Pauline showers all her love and affection on "the little pink-and-yellow girl" (87) when she begins to cry. She reassures the white girl and orders Pecola, Claudia and Frieda to get out of the house. She promises the girl to make another berry cobbler for her while the little girl keeps asking her about the three black girls. The chapter ends with Pauline reassuring the little girl in her mellifluous voice "Hush. Don't worry none." (87) The three girls are driven away mercilessly.

Chapter VII: SEEMOTHERMOTHERISVERY . . .

This chapter begins with an excerpt from the primer about the picture perfect white Mother who is very 'nice' and who 'plays' and 'laughs' unlike Mrs. Breedlove. This chapter fills in details about Pauline Breedlove's life.

Pauline Breedlove was born Pauline Williams and was the ninth of eleven children. She lived in Alabama. When she was two years old, a nail ran through her foot leaving her with a life-long deformity. As a result her foot flopped and caused her embarrassment. She became a quiet introvert girl because of the limp. She was left out of a number of things as no one ever gave much importance to her. She neither had a nickname nor was she ever told any stories that were told to other children. Nobody cared about her favourate things. In short, she never felt at home anywhere. Consequently, she cultivated her own personal pleasures. She gratified herself with organizing things, creating order and neatness out of clutter and being meticulous. She enjoyed housekeeping and liked the silence and solitude of the work.

Her family moved from Alabama to Kentucky at the beginning of World War I. She grew up in a five-room farmhouse as the family's fortunes grew in Kentucky. She left school when she was sufficiently old and took on the responsibility of her two younger siblings called Chicken and Pie on her mother's behalf who worked as a cleaner. Though she enjoyed her work but soon became edgy and sad. She started fantasizing about a stranger who would come and sweep her off her feet. One summer day she met her dream lover and fell in love with Cholly Breedlove. It so happened that Pauline was leaning against her fence after putting some biscuit dough on the oven, Cholly the stranger came up to her whistling. It was love at first sight for Pauline. "For the first time Pauline felt that her bad foot was an asset. . . .

She had not known there was so much laughter in the world." (92) He liked her country ways and he treated her foot as an opportunity to care for her.

Cholly was Pauline's multihued man. When Pauline first saw Cholly, she felt all "the bits of color" (91) rushing down from the memories of her childhood in Alabama—purple of the mashed berries, yellow of lemonade, green of june bugs—deep within her. The colours came together when Cholly tickled her foot. When Cholly made love to her during the early years of their marriage, Pauline describes it as a feeling like "laughing between my legs." (104) Pauline's sexual orgasms were multicoloured. She and Cholly were content and devoted to each other.

The two move to Lorain where Cholly works in a steel mill. Gradually life starts to become more difficult for both of them. Pauline is flabbergasted by the aloofness of the other women who make fun of her country ways, her southern accent, woolly hair, and her makeupless face. Pauline finds the blacks as nasty as the whites. Cholly on the other hand did not have any difficulty finding friends and he often went out at night with them. She begins to yearn for new clothes that would make the women look at her with respect. She and Cholly begin to quarrel about money as Cholly is unhappy with her splurging. Finally Pauline takes up a job as a housekeeper for a white family. Cholly's constant drinking aggravates their marital problem. She remembers them fighting all the time.

One day, Cholly shows up at her workplace drunk and demands money; as a result she loses the job. The white woman refuses to give Pauline the money she owed her unless she leaves Cholly. Pauline refuses as she finds the white woman's argument extremely irrational and having no other option she leaves without the money she needs to pay for cooking gas.

Soon Pauline becomes aware that she is pregnant. Cholly is glad with the news. He begins coming home regularly, cuts back on his drinking and starts taking better care of his family. Pauline stops working and goes back to staying at home again. Cholly and Pauline become affable and their marriage seems to improve once again. But Pauline is still lonely and feels despondent. Pauline begins going to the movies as she has very little to do with herself. This time it is the movies that fill her life with fantasy. It is here that she develops the destructive ideas about physical beauty and romantic love—two of the most destructive ideas in the history of human thought. She starts associating physical beauty with virtue and regards love and romance as the singular goal of a relationship. Captivated by the white society's ideal of beauty, she tries to make herself look like a movie star and tries to style her hair like Jean Harlow. One such day while she is watching a movie and eating a piece of candy, her front tooth falls out. The instance is devastatingly evoked: "Everything went then." (98) She begins to hate herself when she becomes conscious of the reality of her ugliness. Her relationship with Cholly deteriorates rapidly. The fights become more and more brutal.

Eventually she has Sammy who is her first born and then Pecola. When Pecola is in the womb, Pauline talks to her, and is determined to love her no matter what. She feels good about having this baby. When she goes into labour, she hears a doctor tell a group of young doctors that black women do not feel pain while giving birth because they are "just like horses." (*99*) Despite the doctor's rudeness, Pauline is delighted with her new baby but does realize that the baby looks ugly.

Cholly goes back to his drinking. Pauline has nothing to look forward to as last of her tooth falls off.

With two children to take care, she gets a permanent job with the affluent Fishers, who are kind and genial and value her good work. She is delighted in the fantasy-like world of the white family. Pauline loves their house and devotes all her energy in taking care of their home, consequently neglecting her own home. She showers all her love on the Fisher daughter but is rude and insulting to her own children. Life at the Fishers is more contented because there is an abundance of beauty, order, virtue, and because everything is pleasant and unthreatening. She stops taking care of her own house, her children, and Cholly. The chapter closes with Pauline speaking about her unsuccessful marriage to Cholly, and how their lovemaking that turned everything into rainbow colours has become mechanical. Pauline herself becomes indifferent to it and thinks that God will make things better for her one day.

Chapter VIII: SEEFATHERHEISBIGAND . . .

This chapter once again begins with an excerpt from the primer which describes a high spirited father of the perfect white family who is robust and strong. So is Cholly Breedlove. But the similarity ends there. In the primer the father is a loving, doting father who plays with the daughter, Jane. Cholly on the other hand doesn't play with his daughter; instead, he rapes her during one of his drunken stupors.

In this section, the narrator recounts the history of Cholly's life and his background. Cholly was born in Georgia. He was abandoned by his mother who wrapped him up in newspapers and threw him into a junk heap by the railway track. He was only four days old. He was raised by his Great Aunt Jimmy who rescued him. Cholly was thankful to her for saving him, but at times he had his doubts and wished himself dead as she appears senile and irrational. He never did get to learn much about his mother except that in all probability she was insane. His biological father, Samson Fuller, was never around either. When Cholly inquired why she did not name him Samson, Aunt Jimmy told him that there was no reason to do so since he too abandoned Cholly even before he was born. She named him after her brother Charles who was a good man.

Cholly gave up school two years later and took a job at Tyson's Feed and Grain Store. It was here that he met Blue Jack whom Cholly considered his mentor and looked up to him as a father figure. Cholly was fascinated with Blue Jack's stories of Emancipation, ghost stories of white people, women he had been with, fights he had been in, and of his escape from an execution while others were not so lucky. Cholly had fond memories of Blue Jack smashing a watermelon and sharing it with him for a church picnic. For a long long time Cholly remembered this benevolence of Blue Jack.

While Cholly was in his teens his aunt fell sick never to recover again. She died one morning leaving him alone. Cholly's life changes for ever after Aunt Jimmy's funeral. Her funeral was the first Cholly had ever attended and it was here that Cholly met a girl named Darlene. He had his first sexual experience with her, but while they were in the middle of the act they were caught by two white men who derisively laughed at Cholly and forced him to continue. Disgraced and powerless, Cholly had no option. Strangely, Cholly's hatred is directed against Darlene and not the white men who turned tender lovemaking into a voyeuristic spectacle and abused them. He hated Darlene because she was a witness to his impotency, who knew that he did not have the power to protect her.

The humiliation by the two white men destroys the humane side of Cholly permanently. He is supposed to be taken in by an uncle, but he runs away. He is afraid that Darlene might be pregnant and also because he has a deep urge to find his father. He finds Aunt Jimmy's handbag that has twenty-three dollars in it. He finally manages to buy a bus ticket and arrives at Macon. He seeks out his father because he needs to understand himself. He eventually finds his father gambling in an alley and is surprised to see him because he is smaller than he is and is bald on the top of his head. Samson Fuller on the other hand has long since forgotten that he had fathered a son and does not want anything to do with Cholly. Fuller thinks that Cholly has been sent by one Melba whom he owned money. Samson is too immersed with the game of dice to even listen to Cholly. Cholly is not prepared for the insolence and indifference meted out by his father. He is shocked and his resolve shatters. He stumbles back into the street and, in his attempt not to cry, soils his pants. For the first time, he mourns Aunt Jimmy's death: "With a longing that almost split him open, he thought of her handing him a bit of smoked hock out of her dish." (123) The rejection by the father is the final straw in Cholly's life: "Abandoned in a junk heap by his mother, rejected for a crap game by his father, there was nothing more to lose." (126)

For the first time in his life, Cholly feels free, "dangerously free" (125). From that point onwards, he becomes indifferent to everything around him. He hooks up women and knocks them down, takes up jobs and leaves them at his own fancy; he even kills three white men. He becomes absolutely indifferent to all things around him. He seems to take charge of his life and feels "godlike." (126). It is in this self-righteous state of freedom that he meets and falls in love with Pauline Williams. Her charm and naiveté attract him so much that he seems to want to spend the rest of his life with her.

Cholly's abandonment by both his parents plays havoc with his married life. Marriage makes him feel trapped. He initially genuinely loves Pauline but the coming of the children results in a very complicated and confused state of mind. Without any perception of how to raise children, having never known a strong parent-child bond or even enjoyed the basic security of parental love, Cholly counters all family problems according to the temper he's in, never taking into account the emotional needs of his wife or his children. The regularity and repetition of married life sapped his imagination.

He does not know how to be a father to his two children. The responsibility of a father eludes him because he never had a father literally or figuratively. Samson Fuller's rejection of him in favour of a crap game destroys his relations with his children. He wants to love and care for his children but his dangerously free life makes him do otherwise.

One spring afternoon, Cholly comes home drunk and sees Pecola doing the dishes looking very vulnerable. There is an air of hopelessness and helplessness around her. In his inebriated state, she reminds him of the first time he met Pauline, when she is leaning on the fence scratching her foot with her toe. With mixed feeling of attraction and abhorrence, aggravated by guilt, he is drawn towards her. Having never learned any appropriate way to act as a parent for a distressed child, he despises his daughter for loving him and finally gives in to his own selfish desires. Her frailty makes him painfully aware of his failures. Ultimately, feeling worthless and unable to do or provide anything else for her, Cholly rapes Pecola. Pecola faints as a result. Before Cholly leaves her, he wraps a quilt gently around her, in an inadequate gesture that in no way makes up for his violent transgression. When Pecola regains consciousness, she finds her mother staring at her.

Chapter IX: SEETHEDOG . . . .

This chapter opens with that part of the primer which describes Jane playing and having fun with her dog. The chapter describes an old shaggy dog. There is no similarity between the playful, sprightly dog of the white family in the primer and the scruffy dog of this chapter. It tells the story of a self-proclaimed faith-healer, Soaphead Church (Elihue Micah Whitcomb) and gives a detailed description of his character and ancestry. He is a man of mixed race from West Indies who prefers the company of inanimate objects rather than people. He calls them the "The residue of the human spirit" (131). He is repulsed by any type of contact with other people. It is his education that makes him realize that he is a misanthrope, a label he is totally comfortable with. He is revolted by the very distinguishing features that typify mankind—body odour, bad breath, eye crusts, blackheads, moles, blisters scars, cuts, and pimples all agitated his psyche. Ironically, he chooses to place himself squarely in their midst as an analyst and interpreter of dreams. His proficiency in language and self-deception allows him to be a faith-healer for which people come to him asking for basic needs of love, health and money. Consequently, he calls himself a "Reader, Advisor, and Interpreter of Dreams." (130) This gives him the chance to study other people's indiscretion without really getting deeply involved with them.

He "abhorred flesh on flesh." (131) and the very idea of men or women near him disgusted him. This preoccupation takes on a sinister edge and makes him a pedophile who loves to touch little girls. He becomes obsessed with young girls.

His father was half white and half black whereas his mother was half Chinese. She died shortly after childbirth. He was raised chiefly by his father who was an authoritarian schoolmaster.

Soaphead married a woman named Velma. She was a woman who had a zest for life and realized early on that he was determined to remain melancholy. She deserted him promptly. Soaphead, like his ancestors and father, considered education important since this took him a step closer to being white, and a step farther away from one's black roots. Soaphead refined his behaviour and lifestyle that separated him from all things blacks. Along with his revulsion of people, he also abhors dogs, particularly the scruffy old dog of the woman from whom he rents a back room. He even buys poison with the idea of killing the dog himself but is too repulsed to go near it.

At this point, Pecola comes to him with a unique request—to give her blue eyes. Soaphead believes this as "the most fantastic and the most logical petition he had ever received." (137) He is touched by this request because it makes his own desirability to whiteness comprehensible. He sees her as "a little black girl who wanted to rise up out of the pit of her blackness and see the world with blue eyes." (174) He wants to help her. However, his pity for her does not prevent his snatching this opportunity to get rid of the ailing dog. He sees the dog sleeping on the porch and tells Pecola that her desire for blue eyes will be granted if she brings some meat to the dog. He gives her the meat which he has furtively poisoned. She pets the dog on the head and offers the meat but no sooner does the dog eats the meat it dies. Pecola is horrified and runs away crying. Soaphead watches her from the window.

He then sits down to write a very long-winding disjointed letter to God telling Him of His fault in ignoring Pecola. He tells God that he has given Pecola what God Himself failed to do. He has given the girl the blue eyes she so desperately wanted. He adds that no one else will ever see them, except her and she would "live happily ever after." (143) Soaphead is the last nail in the coffin of Pecola's insanity. The letter that he writes reveals the deceptive and dangerous character of Soaphead. He tells God about his dalliance and his predilection for little girls, and specifically, his fascination for their burgeoning breasts. He brags to God that although he has fondled young girls many a time in exchange of sweets and money but he has not touched Pecola who already shows signs of advanced pregnancy. He finishes the letter, seals it and goes to sleep. His landlady arrives to find her dog dead.

Chapter X: SUMMER: I have only to break . . .

This section is narrated by Claudia once again. She reminisces about some of the things she connects with one particular summer—the strawberries, unexpected thunderstorms and tales about Pecola. She remembers a storm her mother told her about that blew away half of South Lorain in 1929. She along with Frieda is selling marigold seeds to earn money in order to buy a new bicycle. They wander all over town even though their mother has advised them only to call on those houses they are familiar with. It is then that they eavesdrop on adult conversations and learn that Pecola has been impregnated by her father. They also learn that only a miracle can save the baby. Claudia and Frieda feel awful for Pecola, all the more because no body else feels so. Claudia wants the baby to live as she "felt a need for someone to want the black baby to live, just to counteract the universal love of white baby dolls, Shirley Temples, and Maureen Peals." (190) It did not bother them that the baby was the outcome of an incestuous rape of Pecola by her own father.

They decided they must do something to help Pecola and make the baby live. They resolve to sacrifice the few dollars they had made by selling the marigold seeds. They bury that money close to Pecola's house as an offering to God. They also put the rest of the marigold seeds in the ground believing that if the marigolds blossom they would know that the baby would live. They parallel the fruitfulness of the earth to the fruitfulness of Pecola. The two sisters sing and pray in the hope that the baby would live.

Chapter XI: LOOKLOOKHERECOMESJANE . . .

Section A

This last chapter opens with an excerpt from the primer concerning a friend who will come and play with Jane. The story is narrated from Pecola's angle. Like Jane, the picture-perfect white girl of the primer, Pecola too has a 'friend' but her friend is imaginary. Pecola's hallucination has produced an imaginary friend for her because she has no real friends. Even Claudia and Frieda now keep away from her.

This chapter is a dialogue between Pecola and her imaginary friend. The friend's voice is in italics. The friend disapproves of Pecola for constantly admiring herself in the mirror. Pecola really considers her eyes to be blue—the bluest eyes in the entire world. She believes her eyes to be so brilliant and luminous that not even strong sunlight can force Pecola to blink and now she can look directly at the sun without any danger of harming her pretty blue eyes. She thinks that her friend and the whole world are jealous of her blue eyes. She fails to see that the real reason people avoid her is because of the shame of incest. Speaking to her imaginary friend, Pecola confides in her that she was the victim of her father's rape on more than one occasion. She tells her that she has told mother about the first occurrence, but she did not believe Pecola, so the next time it happened, Pecola kept it to herself. Her friend insinuates that she enjoyed her sexual encounter with her father which Pecola denies vehemently. It becomes obvious that Cholly has left their home and therefore Pecola no longer has to dread his sexual advances. Her brother Sammy too has left. Through their conversation we also come to know that Mrs. Breedlove no longer speaks to her daughter.

They finally go back to the thrilling discussion about the beautiful blue eyes. Pecola makes her friend reassure her that her eyes are bluer than anybody else's. The section ends with Pecola speculating fanatically whether her eyes are blue enough.

Section B

In the final section we once again return to the first-person narrative of Claudia in the present. Claudia ends the story by telling how she and Frieda occasionally saw Pecola after the baby died a premature birth. Pecola's strange and bizarre behaviour forced people to look away. At times people even laughed at her. Pecola was a complete wreck. She spent her days walking up and down the street believing herself to be a bird, unable to fly and reach the blue sky she has always dreamed of reaching.

Claudia describes Pecola's insanity. It is one of the most painful and disturbing portrayals of madness. She spent her time "walking up and down, up and down, her head jerking to the beat of a drummer so distant only she could hear. . . beat the air, a winged but grounded bird, intent on the blue void it could not reach—could not even see—but which filled the valleys of the mind." (158) Pecola's tragedy was absolute and complete.

As for Pecola's family, Sammy left town, Cholly died in the workhouse, and Mrs. Breedlove continued working for rich, white people. Pecola still lives in a little brown house with her mother. Claudia and Frieda feel guilty because neither did their flowers grow nor did Pecola's baby live.

Claudia realizes that Pecola was the scapegoat of their town and perhaps the entire society. Pecola's unattractiveness allowed all the others to believe they were attractive and blessed. Against her ugliness, everyone felt beautiful. Claudia believes that the only ones who loved Pecola were Maginot Line, the prostitute, and, in a violent, distorted way—Cholly. Unfortunately Cholly's love proved fatal for her as "The love of a free man is never safe." (159) Claudia now realizes that if the marigolds did not blossom it was because "[This] soil is bad for certain kinds of flowers" (160); that with some soil there is no possibility of growth. She becomes conscious that it is too late to help Pecola just as it is too late to bring back the marigolds. Claudia laments "it's much, much, much too late" for Pecola's tragedy is irreversible. By the end of the novel, we find Pecola wandering through the garbage dump, herself a piece of waste.

Writing the Wrong: The Theme of Marginality in Toni Morrison's *The Bluest Eye* and Arundhati Roy's The *God of Small Things*

In "The Second Coming," Yeats writes, "Things fall apart; the centre cannot hold." This 'centering' is the affliction of modernity, and the bane of power discourses. No matter the cause, the margins of this center have fascinated decadent and the dominant groups alike. Marginalization is a slippery and multi-layered concept. The experience of marginality can arise through being born into a marginalized group or acquiring marginality through some personal or structural mishap. It is a major human problem, undermining the essence of humanity. Marginality is an experience affecting millions of people throughout the world. Being poor, unemployed, discriminated, or disabled in a society are serious risk factors. Being excluded from economic, social and political life can have adverse effects on individuals and communities alike.

While in the past, minority literature has merely been included in the academic curriculum, today one of the major features of contemporary literature has been the interest evinced in the marginalized group whose existence is, largely, peripheral. It has become important to recognize the dominant ideologies responsible for the marginalization of minorities. Perceived as lacking essential characteristics possessed by the dominant group, the marginals are usually seen as lesser or inferior beings and treated accordingly. They live in physical or psychological ghettos. Deprived of economic, political or religious power, as they are, they grope in the dark for survival. The social group in which they are imprisoned by custom and tradition builds walls of segregation around them resulting in distance from the 'ir command' power centers. Invariably, these are people who suffer from economic, societal or political impoverishment and find themselves alienated from the mainstream majority. Marginality is a term associated universally to people all over the world where inequality of any kind results in insecurity, injustice and exploitation—leading to the deplorable fate of the downtrodden and the outcasts. They basically have very few legal rights, may be typified as less intelligent, depraved, and most of the time regarded as sub-human.

The most powerful in the society substantially benefit from keeping people marginalized. It is in the interests of the powerful to impose on the less powerful so that they quietly accept their unfair place in society. The dominant group uses these socially constructed different identities as the bases for carrying out discrimination against less powerful members. Arrayed with the centuries-long lies, secrets, degrading myths; brainwashed and mentally conditioned and with a self so pathetically fractured, these marginal class could never free themselves from the ideological snare and could never acknowledge the inherent traits of being both human. They could never attempt to interpret their realities from their *own* point of view and could never establish their *own* priorities or define true objectives. They neither could challenge the multiple oppressions, nor could liberate themselves in the true sense of the word.

The marginalized individual is one who is perceived by the dominant group as not belonging, as being different in some fundamental way and is the Other. The dominant group sees itself as the standard and judges those who do not meet that norm (that is, who are different in any way) as marginalized. This takes many forms, for instance, someone who is of a different race (White vs. non-Whites), a different nationality (Indians vs. Italians), a different religion (Hindus vs. Muslims, Protestants vs. Catholics or Christians vs. Jews), a different social class (aristocrats vs. serf), a different political ideology (capitalism vs. communism), a different sexual orientation (heterosexual vs. homosexual), a different origin (native born vs. immigrant).

The root cause of marginality is inequality, which is a cause for difference, discrimination and exploitation. Marginalized sections of society are generally beyond the pale of the dominant culture. Marginality varies in its degree, extent or intensity. The form and nature of marginality depends upon the degree of impoverishment—economic, social or cultural. Marginality based upon caste, creed, religion or race is a kind of disability or affliction. Most cultures have empowered groups at one end and impecunious (poor) groups at the other and between the two, the people having graded power and poverty. The empowered people enjoy greater degree of freedom, social status and security of life. The impecunious people are not free from fear of uncertainty and injustice.

India and the United States are plural societies with several crosscurrents operating within the nations. Although both the nations are melting pot of cultural diversity, yet in the recorded human history, no other group of humanity has ever suffered from such a socio-economic, physical, cultural and sexual torment and agonies like the blacks in America and the untouchables (dalits) in India. The blacks in America and the untouchables in India are the marginalized and exploited people, their marginality being primarily social and economic. Being black, the African Americans suffered from racism and fell victim to various atrocities at the hands of the white patriarchs. The untouchables in India were denied even the minimum rights as human beings, rendering them incapable of seeing the light of freedom and comfortable living, thanks to the age-old ideology taught to them by the upper castes in India. Economy forced them into drudgery and they had few opportunities to do cerebral work. Through politics of exclusion, they were prevented to have the rights and privileges routinely extended to the members of other groups.

Black American as well as Indian writers in their writings have given expression to the protest against the established order of society that discriminates one man from another on the basis of caste, colour and religion. They envisage a society that is based on new order, a society that values the principles of liberty, equality and fraternity. The success of minority authors has contributed to more than just a resolution of the problem of the marginalization of minority culture. It has brought minority authors a great deal of prestige that has given them access to the inner workings of the literary establishment. For instance, authors such as Toni Morrison, because of her reputation of expertise, have been granted editorial positions. Arundhati Roy as an activist is much more strong, lethal and "within." Now on the "inside," these minority individuals have the power to see that minority literature is published and disseminated to a large sector of the population. In addition, these individuals, able to recognize the cultural heritage that makes these authors' pieces of writing so magnificent, will ensure that this identity is preserved rather than substituted for Western style.

The two novels under review are comparable on various levels. Both depict the social reality of conflict between the powerful and the powerless. If *The God of Small Things* is Roy's first and only novel that catapulted her to the top slot worthy of the Booker, then *The Bluest Eye*, Morrison's first novel, followed by a series of other novels, paved the way for the Nobel Prize. What is remarkable about the two novels is that they are written by women writers who are social activists in their own rights and believe that any writing, novel or otherwise, should not only be aesthetically pleasing but also serve a social or political purpose.

The present article deals with the violation of human values and ethics and the subsequent impasse, which lead to the tragic deaths of the protagonists in both the novels. Caste and colour uncertainty are the leitmotif of the two novels.

While "small things" ironically suggest insignificance, worthlessness, unimportance, triviality etc. *The God of Small Things* depicts all that and much more by way of the marginals in the rigidly caste-structured society in Kerala. Indeed, the novel lays itself down as a testimony to the fragility of the small, marginalized things. According to the Hindu scriptures, there are four main castes performing a function in sustaining the social life in India. *Brahmins* who are the priests; *Kshatriyas*, the warriors and rulers; *Vaisyas* the landowners and merchants; and

Sudras the artisans and servants. *Sudras* have been referred to as Untouchables, Scheduled castes, Harijan and more recently as *Dalits,* a Hindi word which means oppressed or downtrodden. The weaker sections of the society, the have-nots, undeniably suffer a good deal more in the process of caste-stratifications.

Arundhati Roy spectacularly handles the issue of marginality, the effects of subjugation especially on the women, children and the casteless. The idea of untouchability is examined at two echelons in the novel. Firstly, we have social untouchables, who are never allowed basic human rights (Velutha and the likes). Secondly, we have figurative untouchables in high castes (Ammu, Estha, Rahel). Velutha, the god of small things, cannot dream of a peaceful coexistence with the high-caste Hindus and the Syrian Christians because of the stigma of untouchability that is attached to him. Ammu, the female central character, cannot pursue happiness because in so doing she is threatening the existing order, to which society does not take kindly. The powerfuls would seize every possible opportunity to stop these changes. Here discrimination expresses itself in oppressing and exploiting the paravans and the women in their personal and public life. *The God of Small Things* depicts the ways and means that a system adopts to depersonalize an outcaste man or a pariah woman.

Roy develops Velutha to the level of a cataclysmic hero. "Bare bodied" Velutha (*God* 6), a self-made man, is a master craftsman, having no parallel as a carpenter. He is full of life, hope and aspirations, is a Communist worker and takes party activities rather seriously. Firmly placed by caste at the bottom of society, he is aware of its taboos, and yet readily breaks out of these strictures. Since he is looked down upon and maltreated almost at every stage in his life, it becomes his life's mission to change the existing conditions of the society. However, the caste-oriented rigidity plays havoc with his life.

The well-built Velutha creates ripples in lonely Ammu's heart. Velutha and Ammu fall for each other, throwing all scruples of caste and community to the air. This in fact is the beginning of the end for both of them. Vellya Paapen (Velutha's father) and Baby Kochamma (Ammu's Aunt), upon discovering their affair, exhibit a typical indebtedness to their dominant cultural prejudices. As a result Velutha is falsely implicated in Sophie Mol's death and made the villain of the piece. He is badly beaten with batons and boots at the police station where he eventually dies. On the other hand, Ammu's is more than a tragedy. She is humiliated at the hands of her near and dear ones, the police, and shown the door. Even at her deathbed, she is left to herself. Since Ammu lives in a patriarchal culture, she is made to suffer throughout her life.

If *The God of Small Things* is a tale of lost dreams where the dreams are slowly built up and crumble, then *The Bluest Eye* is an inquiry into the reasons why beauty gets wasted. The beauty in this case is black; the wasting is done by white cultural engine that seems to have been designed specifically to murder possibilities; the bluest eye refers to the blue eyes of the blonde American myth, by which standard the black-skinned and brown-eyed always measure up as inadequate. The focus is on the 11-year-old black girl named Pecola Breedlove, who is made to bear the burden of the cosmetic cross. It tells the painful story of Pecola who is obsessed with her desire to become white. Her futile longing for the 'bluest eyes' eventually drives her mad, as she accepts someone else's definition of beauty and loses herself in a hopeless struggle. In this subtle and disturbing early work, Morrison tells an ugly story, creating in the process, a real beauty. Pecola looks fully capable of accepting the idea that socially respected white beauty alone merits love. Her inner drive compels her to become a blue-eyed 'Shirley Temple' and counterbalance her blackness. This is the story of the nightmare at the heart of her yearning and the tragedy of its fulfillment.

Women of colour especially blacks are judged according to white standards of beauty and therefore they are always considered ugly. The black women have shown an irresistible impulse not only for white beauty ideals but also for the white cultural traits. Assimilation into the white culture indicates a desire on the part of the blacks to find entry into the mainstream pattern of living. At its very core is a self-destructive malady. Deeply embedded is the white theory that everything black must be wiped out so that the white self can come into being. It ensures a flight from the Afrocentric cultural roots and an unconditional acceptance of the values of the unachievable Eurocentric world.

Though Morrison wrote this novel at the height of the "Black is Beautiful" era when the blacks were being reconditioned to believe that their looks were synonymous with beauty, Pecola unquestioningly accepts the ideology that white features correlate with beauty. Although beauty is the larger theme of the novel, Morrison scrutinizes the dominant white culture's influence on various levels. Morrison sets the foundation of the novel on issues of beauty in an attempt to make blacks aware that they do not have to conform to white standards on any level.

The novel speaks to the masses, both white and black (brown and yellow as well), showing how a racist social system wears down the minds and souls of people, how dominant images of white heroes with blue eyes and wonderful lives show young black children that to be white means to be successful and happy. The blacks look around at their own lives of poverty and oppression and learn to hate their black heritage for keeping them from the 'Dick and Jane' world. This oppression in many cases led to self-hatred. The blacks felt that all their problems were due to the fact that they had dark skin. The poverty in which they lived and the discrimination they faced caused them to idealize the white race instead of fight for freedom and equality.

Morrison portrays the black community as a society ensnared by its internalization of a 'blue-eyed, yellow-haired, pink-skinned' beauty ideal. Accordingly, blacks learn to hate themselves. Thus, the ideal of beauty becomes a dangerous and racist trap into which the blacks are born, and from which they can never entirely escape. It becomes difficult for people, particularly black female children, to survive the values imposed by the dominant white culture. Pecola is destroyed by the cultural values she adopts. Pecola is very vulnerable to white cultural values, because the more confusing, different, poverty-ridden or depressed a child's life is, the more she will yearn for the norm the dominant society says provides beauty and happiness.

Though the settings of the two novels are very different, yet they are veritable sagas of unending pain, anguish and agony, occasionally punctured by brief moments of hope and relief. In a small space, the authors present a world where certain notions that are regarded as immutable are seen as mobile. Foregrounding race, class and caste position, they ask for an inclusive society, free of the crippling dogma that surrounds it. The novels present the tragic plight of the protagonists victimized at the hands of various exploiters, often times the victimizers being their own kin and kith. Roy manages to 'touch' the reader with Velutha's untouchability as he struggles to internalize his place in the casteist society. Morrison uses her critical eye to reveal the evil that is caused by a society that is indoctrinated by the inherent goodness and beauty of whiteness and the ugliness of blackness.

Literature in isolation is not capable of changing society; nevertheless, the two authors are successful in striking a blow below the belt, albeit in a small space.

NOTES

Roy, Arundhati. *The God of Small Things.* New Delhi: India ink. 1997.

Morrison, Toni. *The Bluest Eye.* New York: Washington Square Press. 1970.

Seeds of Destruction:
The Theme of Incest in *The Bluest Eye*

What turns the protector—whether he be a father, brother, uncle or a grandfather—into a predator? *Incesticide* maketh a marauder! Incest is the most common form of child abuse and is far more prevalent than most people realize. It is a product of a deep-rooted patriarchal gender prejudice. Incest is far too common and it has no respect of person. Like ugliness, misery and poverty, incest is not race specific. It neither has any geographical boundary nor any socio-economic preference. It is found in the poorest homes as it is found in king's palaces. Incestuous homes are filled with fractured people who continue to break themselves and others again and again.

From the time the Greek historians first wrote about the customs and traditions of other countries, researchers have compared the behaviour and practices of different social orders in the hope to determine meaningful cognates in human behaviour. Yet the only universal trait that has been found in every known culture is the prohibition of incest. From the various cultural studies it has been established that no known community has ever sanctioned incest.

Undoubtedly, one of the top taboos still lying around the human race in general, incest is seen as the abuse of a child by a parent or other parental figure or by a more powerful sibling or other relative for the person's sexual gratification. It is sexual relation between two close blood related persons. Incest can be viewed as a form of human attraction which takes precedence over family bond.

Parent-child incest is the most abhorrent as it is an inherent violation of the 'protector' and 'guardian' responsibilities of the parent. The act thus becomes a betrayal of trust the child has reposed in the parent. If on one hand incest tends to emerge in families which have deep-rooted patriarchal gender bias and which look down upon girl child as liability, burden, primarily as sex objects and as commodities which can be bought and sold, then contributing in equal measure are rapidly diminishing human and spiritual values of love, care, sharing, understanding, and forgiveness. Incest is more prevalent in families where the fair sex has no say in the household affairs and is denied space. Men in this atmosphere grow without developing a respect for their mothers and sisters and hence do not hesitate to sexually abuse them and use other forms of control over them. Also working in favour of the abuser is the accessibility of the victim and the belief that he can get away with the crime.

The prevalence of appalling illiteracy, ignorance, backwardness and overtly uncongenial environment, including unhappy and maladjusted violent marital relationships contribute majorly to incest. Incestuous abuse impinges equally on the physical and mental development of the victim. Although there are other types of incest, the father-daughter incest is responsible for 70-90 percent of incestuous relationships.

Experts are of the opinion that one in every three girls is sexually exploited by a family member or someone close to her before she turns eighteen. Every seven minutes in the United States, a child is sexually abused by a close family member.

With its theme of incest, *The Bluest Eye* is a devastating work which unfolds within its scenes the excruciating account of Pecola Breedlove being raped by her father. Many objections have been raised for the reason that in the midst of a beautifully crafted story of a black girl who believes that all her troubles will go away if only she had blue eyes and blonde hair like the white girls, there are appalling mentions to egregious child abuse. The novel has been called blasphemous for its depiction of the stark and brutal visions of rape and incest.

The novel's darkest and most appalling moment occurs when the victim turns a victimizer. The ultimate evidence is the father's vicious and tragic rape of his daughter during a confusing moment of tenderness and hatred, heightened by his drunken stupor and sense of impotence and guilt. He rapes his daughter in a gesture of madness mingled with demented love. A child's need for love is simple and is usually transmitted through a sense of being wanted and ultimately by being protected. The most important job for parents to do is to love their children unconditionally and to make them feel beautiful. Unfortunately Cholly's love harms Pecola the most.

Incest results in aloofness in the victim and tells the victim that (s)he is undesirable and unwanted. Pecola in the midst of her struggle with ugliness and desire for beauty is an obvious casualty. Her innocence and passivity make her an awfully easy prey. She is still a child, but because Pecola is menstruating, she is in the process of becoming a woman; something for which she herself is far from prepared.

The 'Dick and Jane' passage at the beginning of the novel illustrates the difference between a perfect white American family and the warring, wounded Breedloves, who are weighed down with abuse, incest, and racism. The subtitle "Hereisthehouse" is very ironical because the father rapes his daughter in their kitchen which is supposed to be a safe place. A house is supposed to be a place of comfort and security but the incestuous abuse which occurs there twists this definition of a house. It is Pecola's tragedy that she is homeless in her own home which fails to nurture her self. The novel begins with Pecola being in a house, an appalling place fraught with abuse and incest, and ends with her shunning her home and instead living in a safe and secure place of madness.

Morrison makes one fully conscious of the types of possible transgressions that surround all children—filthy glossy magazines, disgusting old men, nasty girls next door, sexual abuse of girls, and above all incest. Morrison portrays adults as preying on children and destroying their innocence. She writes about a victim who is a child who becomes an unwitting pawn for certain kind of 'passive' people who create the situation she is in. Morrison speaks up for a child—one who goes most unnoticed because of the silence she maintains throughout the novel.

Morrison chose to depict the rape from Cholly's point of view and it seemed at times as though Morrison is defending Cholly by describing him as a free spirit and amiable rogue. But is he free to create a way of life out of the chaos he has brought about like the Almighty who created the world out of chaos? There is no excuse for Cholly's action which to say the least was heinous. He cannot be forgiven for what he did to Darlene, Pauline and above all to Pecola. It is not possible to either approve or defend his unspeakable act. Even his past and his own terrible childhood experiences can't justify his actions.

Yet it becomes very important to understand the role played by Cholly's conflicting and inconsistent emotions. Cholly has a whole series of events in his life that make him treacherously free to devour his own hunger. The first sexual experience with Darlene is a turning point in Cholly's life. While in the midst of losing his virginity after the funeral of his Aunt Jimmy, his closest relative, he and Darlene are discovered by two white men. They force Cholly to continue with the act while they abuse him with the choicest of derogatory names and compel him to, "Make it good" (117). Since Darlene is a witness to the humiliation and he cannot direct his hatred toward the men who are humiliating him Cholly turns his rage toward the girl. He acts "with violence born of total helplessness" (116). He is forced to physically rape Darlene, while the two white men psychologically, emotionally, and mentally rape him. The white men turn the act of sex into one of rape. Sex is changed from an act of pleasure and desire into one of hate and control. It is because of this that Cholly continues to act with a similar violence throughout his life. It is painfully obvious that the sexual outrage combined with abandonment (thrown into a garbage bin by his mother and disowned by his father) is the central force in the life of Cholly. These lead him to hate himself and destroy others. His incapability of showing love and feeling are shown through his interaction with those closest to him: his wife and children.

On one hand Pecola's rape has its root in Cholly's humiliating first sexual encounter with Darlene and on the other hand the 'foot image' of Pecola standing on one foot and "scratching the back of her calf with her toe" (127) reminds him of Pauline the first time he saw her and of the time Pauline was attracted towards him. The vulnerability that attracted him to Pauline also attracts him to his own daughter. "The confused mixture of his memories of Pauline and the doing of a wild and forbidden thing excited him," (128) writes Morrison explicitly. He mistakes his lustful desire for pity and love for his daughter. Powerless and confused, Cholly gives into the feeling of protectiveness and tenderness and acting out of anger at himself, similar to the time he displayed anger on Darlene he rapes and impregnates her. This horrendous act is due to the confusion about parental love, its duties and responsibilities because "Having no idea of how to raise children, and having never watched any parent raise himself, he could not even comprehend what such a relation should be" (126).

In no way can we justify what Cholly does. At the same time, Pauline cannot be let off the hook easily. She is equally to be blamed for the incest in the house. Pauline, more than anyone else, knew Cholly's temperament, yet she refused to believe, and protect her daughter from his licentious advances. Moreover she rejects Pecola for becoming pregnant. Pauline's anger is directed at the daughter for it stems from the impossibility of any other kind of action, given her own destitute situation and belief in sexual taboos. Her ruthless detachment actually inflicts a traumatizing emotional and physical isolation upon Pecola.

She had total contempt for Pecola. Pauline sowed the seed of ridicule and shame in Pecola so when she matured instead of blossoming she felt unworthy and shrivelled. Pecola's road to madness had already been paved the day she was born by her mother!

A very crucial aspect of the portrayal of the rape is Pecola's anesthetized mind-set.. Instead of experiencing any sort of emotion, Pecola is in absolute shock and pain when Morrison graphically describes Pecola's intake of breath and Cholly's painful attempt to remove himself from "the dry harbor of her vagina" (128). It is only at the last part that we actually find out Pecola's response to the rape when she is talking to her friend of fantasy: "Horrible" (155).

With her raw, honest, humane portrayals of deranged people, Morrison superbly describes the damage people like Cholly do to their children. They have so little ethical value that their actions can't possibly matter, however much hurtful or otherwise. Cholly's dangerous passion demonstrates how it can result in devastation. He gives himself over to his passions and eventually destroys himself as well as everyone around him. Morrison 'bears witness' to the dangers of potential sexual abuse and incest; she also bears witness to children who are often vulnerable or are silent victims of sexual abuse on many levels. By so doing she is suitably taking on the burden of her responsibility as a black, a woman and a writer.

The novel expresses a very serious issue and causes one to look at society and oneself quite differently. It portrays an extreme instance of the potential consequences arising from such sexual abuse which leave everyone unsettled. The most gut-wrenching part of the novel is that all her life Pecola sought to be noticed. But when she does get noticed, it is by the wrong person with the wrong ideas. Pecola's life is turned upside down with his violation of her. Cholly ends up destroying the psyche of young Pecola. What Morrison presents in *The Bluest Eye* is an extreme view of life with(out) a father.

Dying to Fit in: The Cosmetic Cross in *The Bluest Eye*

Beauty plays a very vital role in a society, and has a huge impact in shaping people's behaviour. Beauty has always been categorized under outer appearance. But true beauty isn't all about physical traits a person has; true beauty lies within an individual. Men and women of all ages and races spend time, money, and energy to try their hardest to bring out their outer beauty in order for them to impress others, but spend little or no time shaping their inner beauty—their true beauty. Physical appearance does bring happiness but true happiness is found when an individual is happy because they accept who they are and not the ideas impressed upon them by society on the way they should look. Removing your imperfection can cause you to die, literally or hypothetically.

Beauty is skin deep, yet the effect that beauty has on individuals who consider themselves less than perfect is incredible. Beauty has been a problem for years because from time immemorial writers have written about how society defines beauty as a physical appearance. The five most retold fairy tales like *Cinderella, Snowhite, Little Red Riding Hood, Hansel and Gretel and The Sleeping Beauty* give non-whites, especially black girls, the harmful impression that it pays to be pretty. Almost all the stories concentrate on looks, particularly female beauty. The stories contain so many stereotypes that they are all harmful as the lurid sexual images contained in today's popular music videos. From early childhood, girls read fairytales about princesses who achieve vast riches simply because their beauty makes them special. This is a powerful message which inhibits girls who feel they do not meet society's expectations of what it means to be attractive. The message that these fairytales contain is not that you need to be good but that you need to be beautiful. Obviously, beauty continues to have an impact in today's society.

Toni Morrison sets the foundation of *The Bluest Eye* on the issue of beauty in an attempt to make her own sisters (by her own admission she writes specifically for the blacks) aware that they do not have to conform to white standards on any level. Morrison's perception of beauty and attractiveness is that, "a thing of beauty is a joy for ever" and that "beauty is truth." It is very important to remember the specific place from where Morrison, the African American woman writes—the place that is conditioned by the specificity of her own sexual and cultural position in a racist and sexist society. Once we do this, we start noticing that the novel is basically a *black* woman's assessment of black American situation from the perspective that is fully her own. African Americans with their African features, have always had an uneasy coexistence with the European ideals of beauty and compared to males, females have been more profoundly affected by the prejudicial fallout surrounding issues of skin color, facial features and hair. Such impact can be attributed to the importance of physical attractiveness for all women.

The Bluest Eye calls into question the very belief which is rigid, prejudiced and politically motivated. It depicts the force of beauty from the perspective of those who are not included in its traditional definition and suggests alternative concepts of beauty, consequently challenging the conventional, stable notions of universal beauty. Morrison demonstrates clearly the negative effect of beauty that is controlled and defined by a dominant group in society. It is a story that particularly shows the ongoing problems affecting the black race. The story is about cultural beliefs. This story transmits patterns and problems that have a negative impact on the black girls. It not only shows these patterns and problems but also shows how they go unresolved because people just accepted this way of life. The major issue in this novel is the idea of ugliness. The conviction that black is neither beautiful nor valuable is one of the cultural hindrances that blacks have had to face throughout their history in America.

Set in the author's girlhood hometown of Lorain Ohio, *The Bluest Eye* tells the painful story of an eleven-year-old Pecola Breedlove who is obsessed with her desire to become white. She prays for her eyes to turn blue so that she would be beautiful, people would look at her and that her world would be different. This is the story of the nightmare at the heart of her yearning and the tragedy of its fulfillment. Morrison tries to convey that beauty is misunderstood by several societies. She says that "Beauty was not simply something to behold; it was something one could do." There can be no happy ending to a story where a child is not only being rejected by society but rejected by her own parents and her people, those who should have loved and protected her from the cruel world of racism and revulsion. She doesn't have any escape from this mean and malicious world, not a moment where she can have a share of love from someone and dwell in it. This novel shows her rejection and sadness and how it came into existence. In the autumn of 1941, the year the marigold in the Breedloves' garden did not bloom but Pecola's life did change—in a painful, devastating ways. Basically the novel focuses on three young girls: Pecola and her peers, Claudia and Frieda MacTeer. Claudia serves as the narrator and summarizes the plot: Pecola was raped by her father, became pregnant with a child that died, and went insane.

Pecola's parents, Cholly and Pauline, send their daughter to live with the MacTeers because their own home has been destroyed in a fire Cholly started. Claudia and Frieda sense how much Pecola's sensibilities have been shaped by the standards of white American culture: Pecola falls in love with the MacTeers's Shirley Temple mug, drinking three quarts of milk in a single day in order to continue admiring it, and she confides that she prays every night that God will give her blue eyes, which she considers the epitome of beauty. Pauline thinks much like her daughter does, considering the feelings and property of her white employers more important than those of her own family. Cholly, the product of a broken home, cannot come to terms with Pauline's expectations and his own desires. Other members of the community, including Geraldine, a neighborhood black woman, and Soaphead Church, a West Indian religious leader, express similar feelings of self-hatred. While she is living with the MacTeers, Pecola begins to menstruate and to explore her sexuality. Unfortunately after she returns home, Cholly assaults her while she is doing the dishes. Pecola retreats further and further from the real world into madness, finally coming to believe that she has attained her wish for blue eyes. Claudia concludes the novel by revealing that Pecola has become a homeless beggar.

Morrison tells an ugly story of an incestuous rape of Pecola by her father, creating a real beauty in the process. The girl's need to be loved takes the doomed form of a yearning for blue eyes. All the tragedy in this novel can be directed back to one main issue i.e. whiteness as a standard of beauty. This epidemic this illness, this belief that white sets the standards for beauty, is a major factor to the self-loathing which occurred in America in the past as well as today. In America the standard is blonde, blue-eyed, white-skinned girl with regular features. It is a well-documented fact that blue eyes, blonde hair, fair skin are symbols of beauty valued in the west—as emphasized by romantic novels, movies, bill boards and dolls. For Pecola the blue eyes and creamy complexion are the paragon of virtue and as she is black, she negates herself and feels inferior even in her own eyes. The girl who is black has no option in the matter of how much she will change herself. However beautiful she might be in different standards in the country she is ugly.

All the characters suffer most from this farcical standard of beauty and seem to be asking themselves forever as to what makes one love. Beauty? Does it comprise blonde hair, blue eyes and lips and nose of a certain shape? In the novel this theme is given the central place, and the novel sees the fate of black people depending on family relationship and community relationships built upon love and fellow-feeling. The novel states that only love can give true stability to the Black American psyche and give it a sense of identity.

Beauty is something that a lot of people in life strive for. But what most people don't realize is that beauty is in the eye of the beholder. Beauty should not be characterized by what people are told it is, beauty is different for everyone, what is beautiful for one may very well be ugly for someone else. Pecola fails to understand that beauty is not skin deep but encompasses a woman's feeling about herself, her carriage, her style and her heritage. True beauty is a synthesis between physical and personality attributes. Pecola's destiny is ultimately determined by the myth of beauty and value connotations it embodies. But one has to understand the core of that myth and the damaging influence of white culture and values on the lives of black people. Indeed the novel is as much about the plight of Pecola as it is about the collective internalization of self-hatred, the cultural segregation of a people and their mostly unconscious battle with what western civilization considers beautiful.

The novel chronicles the search for beauty among the limitations of life, both from within and without. It documents the destruction of a young girl whose final push to insanity comes after her father rapes her. Pecola yearns for blue eyes as the next best thing to being white. She seeks the glory of blue eyes through prayer and eventually through madness believing that blue eyes have finally been granted to her. Secure in her madness, she has no knowledge that she has become the town pariah. The novel very analytically focuses on and evaluates the processes and symbols of imprinting the self during childhood and what happens to the self when the course of action is lop-sided and the symbols flawed. Morrison shows how idealised images of feminine beauty depersonalise a woman, how the impact of these images is enormously exaggerated in all walks of life and how oppressive they are to the black woman who cannot even aspire to the white ideals that surround her. The novel shows the tragic outcome of those who attempt to escape reality (here blackness) by an unrealistic and self-destructive yearning for the symbols (the blue eyes) and privileges of whiteness or by renouncing their historical identity in order to be accommodated into the white world. *The Bluest Eye* reveals the inversion of the order that results in a black girl's belief that she possesses the greatest treasure, the bluest eyes imaginable. The novel is a patterned fabric in which the warp is the myth of beauty and desirability in a dominant society itself, while the woof is the personal history of hapless Pecola.

Pecola heaps damnation upon herself by making wrong choices and one is led to realize what it means to succeed in a white, racist but somewhat open society. Pecola's quest for affection goes awry. She hungers for love and affection but fails to find it at home, at school and in the community. She is just like Cinderella in the sense that she wants to be something different than what she is naturally. Just like Cinderella, Pecola resorts to fantasy in her own mind. Like Cinderella, who is transformed from a char girl next door, to the belle of the ball, the ugly duckling into beautiful swan, the sleeping beauty for her prince to awaken her, Pecola longs for blue eyes, so that she can become worthy of not any prince charming but of her own parents, her classmates, teachers and many more. Unlike Cinderella and all the other fairytales, this fantasy that Morrison weaves is loaded with the harsh realities of African American life.

The name of the novel itself is highly reflective of the significance placed on blue-eyed little girls. Pecola and her family are the representative of the larger black community, and their name, 'Breedlove,' is ironic. They breed anything but love. In fact, they breed hate—hatred for blackness, and thus of oneself. If whiteness is used as a standard of beauty or anything else, then the value of blackness automatically diminishes. When Mr. Henry addresses the MacTeer girls, "Hello there. You must be Greta Garbo, and you must be Ginger Rogers," the names ring of beauty that the girls will never reach. Black children cannot escape the pervasive presence of the dominant society's cultural icons of female beauty, e.g., Shirley Temple, Jean Harlow, Ginger Rogers, Greta Garbo, Hedy Lamarr, and Betty Grable. The ideal of beauty has been largely depicted as a woman with light skin and blue eyes. It is true that beauty is the central focus of many women but the standard of beauty that Pecola and her peers subscribe to is obnoxious. *The Bluest Eye* powerfully demonstrates how negative values are true only when we ourselves validate them.

The Bluest Eye shows that many people depend on the world to find their self-value and their self-worth which is an inescapable ontological problem. Human relation revolves around the experience of 'the look', for being 'seen' by another both confirms one's reality and threatens one's sense of freedom. This holds a lot of truth in Pecola's life. She looks at others to figure out how she should be feeling and what others see of her, she sees in herself. She thinks that she is ugly, by others' opinions of her, and want to become beautiful so she will be recognized and be the center of attention.

Environment and surroundings always affect our ways of thinking, and also determine who we will become in the future. Passing for white is a phenomenon that captivates Pecola who cannot possibly pass for white, yet she ignores biology and becomes (if only to herself) a blue-eyed Shirley Temple. Pecola completely internalizes the view of beauty as white, blonde, and blue-eyed. At the end of *The Bluest Eye*, Pecola spends her days walking the streets bobbing her head to the beat of a distant drummer with "her arms like a bird in an eternal, grotesquely futile effort to fly" (204). In trying to attain the ideals of a society that is culturally different, Pecola destroys in herself that which is unique to her first as a person, second as a black person. The marginalization and the devastation of Pecola are grounded in superficiality. Her mother, her father and the black community thought that she was ugly, so they ignored her, hated her, and regarded her as an outsider in their society. All of these gross absurdities heaped upon Pecola finally culminate in her madness. Basically Pecola is totally entrapped by everything, her past (rape, incest etc.), her present (society both black and white) and her future (she has very little hope at being a contributing member of society). The novel is an indictment of warped values and twisted lives and is Morrison's most blatant testimony to the impossibilities of love in a world of superficiality.

The novel reveals the evil that is caused by a society that is indoctrinated by the inherent goodness and beauty of whiteness and the ugliness of blackness. It explains the possible consequences of entirely depending on external conditions for self-image, for in attempting to satisfy a paradigm that differs so radically from reality. This leads to the destruction of one's own essential moral fibre. The novel is an attack on the impossible Western cultural ideals imposed on the poor, and especially the non-white. Morrison seems to want to convey the idea that the destructiveness of blacks is more because of their own kind. While racial discrimination and white oppression undoubtedly give rise to certain kind of behaviour in the oppressed, it can't be used as an excuse. In the end, we all have choices. Claudia rejects the very idea that white equals beauty. She hates the white baby dolls, and is confident in her own self-worth. One can choose to reject destructiveness rather than embrace it, if one wants to. Unfortunately Pecola comes from a warped, perverse family, who thereby shapes her perceptions and thoughts about her own life. She has done no wrong, but the failings of her parents to come to terms with their own suffering make Pecola's agony agonizing. *The Bluest Eye* condemns the very notion of beauty and the politics of supremacy behind it; also it is intended as a caution story to the blacks and human beings in general, not to emulate the example of Pecola. She fails to understand that one is as beautiful as one feels. Beauty associated with harassment and humiliation can neither be a source of joy, nor can it be true. To know a person one must look inside one's heart, not at one's face.

No doubt the novel is extremely heart-wrenching but the most tragic facet lies not within the novel. The real misfortune lies in the fact that the underlying injustice, cruelty, and sheer hatred presented in a book written in the 1970s still rings loud and clear today. The out-of-the-way events that unfurl in Morrison's small town of Ohio have a far deeper inference. Such inherent abuse, mistreatment, discrimination, and above all the rape of one of the most vulnerable members of society persist even today unchecked almost sanctioned well into the 21st century.

Toni Morrison's Narrative Approach: A Journey from Realism to Postmodernism

SHAIL BALA
Res. Sch., Jai Prakash University, Chapra

In the second decade of the twentieth century, it had almost become apparently clear that the age-old socio-cultural and ethical norms are on the brink of collapse. This was the reason that T.S. Eliot seems to be crying against the pitiable condition of the humanity and W.B. Yeats was advocating that 'Things fall apart, the centre can not hold.' This was not an abrupt development. Even in the Victorian time, Carlyle, Comte and Ruskin raised their voices against intellectual and moral anarchy. In 1930s, we feel and find that a socio-ethical alternative has been projected to wipe out the anomalies prevailing in the then mode of the society. The thinkers and philosophers speculated in the light of historical, sociological and Marxist perspectives so that the better human condition can be created or the reality of the situation can be understood. Widely and wittingly, it should be understood that literature cannot be a moral preaching and that way it cannot pave the path for ideal human situation. This was the time when it had been declared that modernity has ceased and postmodern modernity has started. Gradually, when we enter 1960s and 1970s, we find that the society is badly divided in the name of class, colour and culture. The United States of America had become the most potent force to spread its racist concept of culture and philosophic nation. A critic like David Lyon argues, "From nineteenth century Romantic reactions to twentieth century postmodernism, questions are raised about the desirability and utility of the modern legacy. One outcome is Nihilism, with its many faces; helplessness, complacency, jouissance, ethical questing and so on."[1] This is the socio-cultural backdrop against which Toni Morrison writes and talks about the modernistic urges and requirements in the postmodernistic flow of time. It is a matter of investigation and analysis that Morrison is not going to offer a challenge against the modernism; rather she is making an effort to search the positioning of the black society in general and the condition of women in particular amid the sexist culture. The viewpoint of Helen Cixous is befitting to understand the critical condition of the women in general which has been marshalled by Morrison. She says, "I detect meaning. Feminine pleasure, enjoyment, may be counter hegemonic in the serious sense that human fulfilment is no longer restricted to male definition."[2]

The African American literature is treated to be an independent branch of literary sensibility and subject, a bit different from American literature. There is a group of critics who consider African American literature as a part of African literature but in theme, theory and contour it is different from original African literature. At the same time, the African Americans have to face odds and obstacles on two fronts, firstly it has African roots, secondly it is struggling to fit well in the channels of American literary heritage. Consequently, we come across a very distinctive phenomenon in Morrison's narrative art. Throughout the world, it has ever been a socio-psychological problem to get one one's colour according to the given scene and circumstances. This is one of the primal reasons that the diaspora literature came to centre-stage in which we find a fighting and crusading mood of the writers for seeking security and stability at the second place where they inhabit. Moreover, Morrison's case is not peculiarly different from diasporic case and context though her creative domain is powerfully dominated by the problems like colour, creed, gender bias, patriarchal domination as well as conflicting puzzlements.

The origin and growth of the African American literature on literary map becomes an outlet for the unquenched human urge and anxiety for freedom and for freedom of expression. Slavery and savagery can be treated as the fertile factors for literary discourse and analysis. No doubt, it offered a conducive contour for the making of a new literature that was produced by the oppressed and that indicated the oppressors. It is a literature of suffering and survival, struggle for freedom and search for identity. It exquisitely records victors and vanquisheds, fears and dreams of their creators. This is now being opposed in and through the works of the Black American women writers in general and Morrison in particular. It is a well-acknowledged fact that women can be more detached and objective to probe into the oppressive and exploitative socio-cultural milieu which marginalized women and their desires and aspirations. Morrison has formulated this kind of judicious approach to peep into the heart of the matter around which life flourishes and functions. The Black women writers like Alice Walker, Paule Marshall, Gloria Naylor, Toni Cade Bambara cover a long span of their writing in which there are different shades and contexts. Stokely Carmichael and Charles V. Hamilton suggest their opinion about these black writers: "The adoption of the concept of Black Power . . . is a call for black people in this country to unite to recognize their heritage, to build a sense of humanity. It is a call for Black people to begin to define their own goals, to lead their own organizations and to support those organizations. It is a call to reject the racist organization and values of this society."[3]

The term 'Black Power' was coined and came in currency during the Civil Rights movement. The Civil Rights Acts of 1964 and 1968 prohibited discrimination on the level of race, sex and class. Racism, sexism and classism provide troublesome and tormenting condition under which African Americans resided in white America. The Black women in America being at once black, female and poor, having been suppressed and subjugated at the hands of the white people and also from the men of the Black world. As a matter of fact, black women are bearers of what Barbara Smith calls, "geometric oppression."[4] Hence the black women are the bearers of the triple consciousness—colour, culture and context. As the Marxists suggest, only the material interests of the dominant class determine our existence, be it legal, economic or cultural order of patriarchal phase of human history. There are also three important socio-cultural aspects related to the literary landscapes of Morrison. At first she is black, secondly she is a woman and thirdly she has settled down in America which is dominated by the racist culture. The conceptual paradigm of the study is that a woman suffers at so many levels. She becomes the victim equally at the hands of the black people as well as the white people. From pillar to post, there is only one voice that is the voice of the selfhood or the identity.

In the changing scenario, the entire social perspective has been characterized into two sets by the great linguist Antonio Gramsci which is very befitting to the study and analysis of the novels of Morrison. He rightly says that the first part of the statecraft is meant for suppressing the subject but in the second part of it, the statecraft shows its humanistic attitude towards the welfare of the society. The very first part of approach is called war of movement and the second part is called war of position. Morrison's creative spectrum covers both the dimensions and exposes vehemently the 'salad' characters of the American mechanism of ruling and exploiting. It is not unfair to say that the novelist has exhibited her sagacity to focus the real sexist and racist character of the American society. As a result of the effort of writers and scholars like Toni Morrison, Alice Walker and Barbara Smith, African American literature has now come to be taught in white universities in the U.S.A. Toni Morrison in her influential lectures collected in *Playing in the Dark* (1991) candidly argues that American or White American literature cannot be understood fully without understanding the black presence or even the absence of blacks in it. She compelled the whites to feel the black presence in American literature.

Morrison, at her best, makes a subtle observation and her narrative cosmos suggests that she has managed to apply her own mode of literary representation. Her themes are close to naturalist fiction—the burdens of history, the determining social effects of race, gender or class. Blacks were viewed from the white standards of life and beauty and this makes blacks' life a kind of unbearable burden. In case of Black women, sexism becomes a weapon for both physical and mental exploitation and the tragedy with black women is that they were sexually oppressed by both black and white men. By facing racial and sexual oppression, the black woman has no friends but only accountabilities and problems. This is the reason that African women could not achieve the standard of womanhood on the one hand and on the other, they were biologically and naturally females, so all the societal and cultural restriction were associated with them. The perusal of black women's lives suggests that to be black and female is to suffer from the duality of racial and sexual discrimination. As a matter of fact, racism and sexism are presented as a licensed weapon for the oppression of blacks. Gloria Wade Gayles arguably provides this interesting phenomenon of inequality through the imagery of circles. There are three major circles of reality in American society, which reflect degrees of power and powerlessness. There is a large circle in which white people, most of them men, experience influence and power. Far away from it, there is a small circle, a narrow space, in which black people, regardless of sex, experience uncertainty, exploitation and powerlessness. Hidden in this second circle is a third, a small dark enclosure in which black women experience pain, isolation and vulnerability. These are the distinguishing marks of black womanhood in white America."[5]

Here, we visualize the encroaching and all-embracing face of racism imposed upon the lives of all blacks irrespective of sex and class. At first in order to enrich their coffers and use their labour, the white masters brought the first Africans in chains. And this way racism started in America. Even today the black people cease to exist as a proper human being on the parameter of white-coloured people. In an influential and illuminating study of the germination of racism in the United States, Joel Kovel argues that the white master "first reduced the human self of his black slave to a body and then the body to a thing; he dehumanized his slave, made him quantifiable and thereby absorbed him into a rising world market of productive exchange."[6]

The roles of blacks have been carved out and formulated by whites and all that was left to blacks was their African soul which was also taken away by imposing white values on them. A sense of inferiority is cultivated by the white people to deprive blacks of their genuine guts and power. In fact, in this process, 'black' and 'female' were juxtaposed against 'white' and 'male'. The focal point of observation and examination is that the entire African American people were condemned to suffer endlessly but the black woman's situation was more piteous and problematic than the black man's condition: "To be black and female was to be in double jeopardy."[7]

Despite all these racial and sexual atrocities, class-exploitation becomes a primary source of oppression of blacks in white America. And it is also a fact that racism is a by-product of capitalism. Capitalism believes in a class-divided society. Primarily, Africans were enslaved for economic reasons, so that their labour power could be exploited. Capitalism, racism and sexism have been so interrelated in the history of America that it is not surprising when black women like Paule Marshall, Alice Walker and Toni Morrison have written novels which reflect that mingling either inwardly or outwardly. As a novelist, Morrison continued this tradition with all her novels. She was born and bred up amidst African culture and heritage, so she exactly and elegantly employed the sense of race, gender and class in her narratology but her argument or emphasis differs from novel to novel.

Morrison's theory of fiction-writing is a kind of reformative and suggestive approach through which she makes us aware of the existing and excruciating condition of the contemporary society. It is an eye-opening fact for the world that America has become a super power for influencing the world in every respect and on the other hand the inner socio-cultural condition and construct of the American society is racially and culturally compartmentalized. Morrison as a narrative artist is a product of these circumstances and all these aspects are seemingly reflected by her narrative art. The study of her novels can be classified in a chronological order so that the growing maturity and the artistry of the novelist can be discerned and discussed. It is a revealing fact for the readers of Morrison that she proved to be the foremost African American woman novelist today but she never wanted to become a writer in her lifetime. Morrison started writing as a therapeutic means of dealing with loneliness when she divorced her husband and lived in Syracuse. Psychoanalytically, 'the unconscious is structured like a language.' In the Lacanian pattern of thought, the 'Phallus' suggests the symbol of power though it has been opposed by the Feminists. But Toni Morrison strongly believes that the African American society is phallic or male-centred in its nature and character. The theoreticians analyse the social conditioning and circumstances in Freudian framework and correlate it with a linguistic transaction. This is the crucial factor that shaped the creative vision of Morrison as a novelist. She professes: "I realized in the process of *The Bluest Eye* that writing had become a compulsion so I become a writer. . . . I will always be a writer."[8]

In her first novel *The Bluest Eye* (1970), the thrust area of interpretation is racism. Pecola Breedlove, the protagonist, suffers from beginning to end mainly because she is black. She becomes a scapegoat of western standards of beauty and love. By presenting Pecola as a scapegoat, Morrison is actually indicting the society as a whole. The scapegoat motif becomes clearer when the victimized Pecola is judged by the society in which she resides. In *The Bluest Eye*, all the characters have accepted white standards of beauty. They are divided selves but they are very much conscious of their blackness as a stigma. Indubitably, colour consciousness is a constant presence in the text, and Morrison works out with this idea and its devastating effects on a poor black family, ironically called Breedlove. In this family, father Cholly Breedlove, mother Pauline, son Sammy and most of all, daughter Pecola lived in luckless and loveless condition.

The Bluest Eye explores and examines the tragic lot of a poor black girl not only for blue eyes but for the bluest of all. The title embodies the facts that the blacks have absorbed the sense of competitiveness as well as the white standards of beauty symbolized by blue eyes. The ultimate standard of beauty compares as "white American prescription for beauty include blonde hair, white skin and above all, blue eyes." Pecola's tragedy in life is closely attached with her mother's miserable conditions. She works as a maid-servant in a white family and she hates the ugliness of her house and her family. Pauline fails as a mother in her inability to bring her child as a loved one. The racial discrimination in which Pecola and her parents are placed and positioned becomes the leitmotif of the novel which is classified into four chapters named after four seasons—autumn, winter, spring and summer. These seasonal classifications assist the reader to understand the recurring images of life of the blacks in white America. There is no ray of hope and happiness for Pecola. "Pauline loves Pecola, but she beats her. Cholly loves Pecola, but he rapes her." Even the marigolds planted by Claudia fail to bloom that signifies the utter hopelessness of the situation. For Pecola, the blue eyes become a panacea for all her ills and evils. At last, Pecola believes having blue eyes means having everything—love, respect, goodness and acceptance and in short truly enviable place in the society. But ironically, Pecola's story is not the usual story of birth, death and rebirth; rather it is a story that moves from pathos to tragedy and finally to madness.

Like *The Bluest Eye*, her second novel *Sula* (1973) focuses on two women and their friendship. Sula and Nel's relationship does not degenerate into a lesbian relationship. Unlike Gloria Naylor and Alice Walker, Morrison considers friendship as the spiritual and emotional bond based on sincere and sensible grounding. Nel is a traditional woman whereas Sula represents the concept of a new woman. The novelist presents them not contradictory but complementary to each other. Here, Morrison is interested to offer the black woman as an individual, struggling for liberty and equality as we find in Alice Walker's *Meridian*. Sula and Meridian are "spiritual sisters" and what they have in common is "intense desire to give birth to themselves as person."[9] Sula develops her intense friendship with Nel at the age of twelve. They become both the sides of the same coin. Morrison creates an unusual world in the novel. Sula, her mother Hannah and grandmother Eva Peace live in a place called Bottom but the irony with the place is that it is up in the hills. Sula is born in a family where the women reign supreme and Eva and Hannah act as role models to Sula. They live in a world which they have created and the result is that Sula rejects the ties and taboos that bind the people in Bottom. Like Cathy-Heathcliff relationship in *Wuthering Heights*, we find that Nel feels that she is more Sula than Nel herself. For Sula, what is more important in her life is the friendship she had nurtured and developed with Nel in a world that preferred disintegration and discrimination.

With the passage of time, Morrison seems to be more mature regarding the relationship between racism, classism and sexism in her third novel *Song of Solomon* (1977). Class plays a key and crucial role in relation to race and gender. Thematically, the story revolves around the male protagonist who has unique and symbolic name like Milkman Dead. *Song of Solomon* is primarily based on the African American folktale about the oppressed African who flew back to Africa to escape the stigma of slavery. The story tells the saga of a black family—Macon Dead, his wife Ruth Foster and their children. Milkman's quest for identity has become the chief concern and the principal obstacle he must overcome is the deadening effects of his father's need to acquire much property so that he may protect himself from the shackles of racism. Morrison not only focuses on the relationship of gender and class in *Song of Solomon* but she also interconnects that concern into her major theme and content. There are two important women characters in Milkman's life—those are Ruth, his mother and Pilate, his aunt who are temperamentally contrasted with each other. If Ruth is a socially committed lady, Pilate has fully rejected the social ethics. In fact, the role of women in the novel becomes an axis where Milkman's consciousness develops and matures into race and gender. Actually speaking, Pilate's role is fully responsible for Milkman's developing consciousness. Michel Foucault, the French critic, is of the opinion that "power is immanent in all social relations and that all social relations are relation of power, whether in a family or in the layers of Government and others social institutions."[10] In his brilliant work *Madness and Civilization*, he suggests that there was a time when the humanity faced "free terror of madness" but the present era echoes the 'stifling anguish of responsibility.' Morrison's fictitious urge champions this concern of Foucault in wider framework.

In a nutshell, Milkman becomes the epitome of self-centredness, heartless and insensitive behaviour towards women. Being trained under the guidance of his father that money is everything, Milkman does not cherish human relationship. Milkman's relationship with his aunt Pilate is coloured by his own fascination. Milkman also treated Hagar, his beloved, in a typical macho manner. The heart-stricken treatment breaks Hagar's heart and she dies a wretched death. But sadly, Milkman fails to find the tragedy and the sense of sacrifice implicit in Hagar's tragic death. In *Song of Solomon*, we get a group of women who put themselves fully and completely for the service and welfare of their men but in return they receive only torture and torment. At last, we realize that Milkman has been transformed into a man who has accepted his fault and ignorance. However, it is pointless to pinpoint that such a realization and identification are enough, Milkman must understand the general oppression of African people in the name of race, class and gender.

The very title of her fourth novel *Tar Baby* (1981) is based on a folktale which decentred the prevalent Euro-American mythology. In the pattern and paradigm of the preceding three novels, Morrison's commitment to *Tar Baby* is to explore the quest for wholeness. This quest is conducted in a setting that is the Caribbean Island which is dominated by the white's presence. Through the Caribbean setting, Morrison is able to suggest the current and cross-currents of different cultures. The novel beautifully depicts the emerging class consciousness of Toni Morrison. Valerian Street is a symbol of American capitalism. He lives with his wife, Margaret, along with their black servants, Sydney and Ondine. Valerian is a typical capitalist who severely exploits the labour of the African people for his pleasure and profit. He treats and tortures human beings only by non-human values like wealth and status. It is true that the ruling class in the United States controls the means of production as Marxism suggests. But it is also a fact that there are some blacks who show the white ideology and their behavioural patterns. Ideologically, it is apparent that Jadine, a tar baby not only thinks like a European but also feels like a European. Unlike Jadine, Son represents the black culture and consciousness. He deeply thinks that if African people in general are exploited, then he too is exploited. Primarily, the novel reflects the novelist's growing class consciousness but unfortunately she fails to offer a viable solution for the oppression of blacks in white America.

Unlike her previous novels, Morrison's Pulitzer Prize winning novel *Beloved* (1987) focuses on the historical truth that the collective struggle is the only solution for African people to wipe out the evils of slavery. The novel deals with the life of a slave mother, Sethe, who kills her own daughter to rescue her from the suffering and horror of slavery. Morrison herself asserts that "the book was not about the institution Slavery with a capital S. It was about those anonymous people called slaves. What they do to keep on, how they make a life, what they are willing to risk, however long it lasts, in order to relate to one another—that was incredible to me."[11] As a slave, Sethe develops awareness about her own subhuman status on the Sweet Home Plantation which ultimately compels her to develop a search for identity. Ironically, the Sweet Home Plantation is neither sweet nor a Home which has bought Sethe to replace Baby Suggs. In Sweet Home, black is being treated in no way different from animal. Surprisingly enough, the novel deals with the death of Beloved who mysteriously reappears as a young lady and claims her mother's love. On a socio-psychological plane, *Beloved* is a story of Sethe's struggles for social freedom and psychological wholeness. She fights with the haunting memory of her slave-past and the retribution of Beloved, the ghost of her baby whom she has killed in order to save her from the life-in-death consequences of slavery. The thematic force and fervour in *Beloved* is immense and perpetual. Actually, Morrison interweaves racial and sexual issues with the theme of motherhood and examines them on socio-psychological and mythical levels. What Morrison has worked out in *Beloved* is extraordinarily effective.

As the very title of her next novel *Jazz* (1992) suggests, Morrison has adopted a unique narrative style in which she has used the mode of Jazz to portray the experiences of the black people during the 1920s, the decade which is known as the Jazz Age. In Morrison's creative outburst, "*Jazz* becomes a multi-perspective novel in which the narrator and the characters become like performers in a Jazz band, each taking a turn to improvise upon his/her respective part and merging into the basic theme or composition."[12] The novel beautifully presents the story of the Joe Trace and her wife, Violet. Both of them lead their life with the troubles and traumas of their past experiences. As the novel proceeds, we find that the black people receive a jolt when Joe Trace kills his beloved Dorcas. And at her funeral, Violet disfigures the face of Dorcas with a knife. Morrison further carries the tradition and gives a refreshing touch to black experience in the novel. The energizing life-giving force of Jazz originates from mystery, continues with surprises and ends in a sense of renewal.

As Morrison is fully committed to the black people in white America, she uses her fictional art as a framework for posing various solutions to the African's oppression on the level of race, gender and class. In *Jazz*, the emphasis is on the unity of women as a solution to gender oppression. The idea of women coming together as a result of gender bias may not be a new idea in Morrison's canon but as Mbalia suggests, "it is a Jazz melody plucked anew and given prominence by the musician who is Morrison."[13] In *Jazz*, Morrison continues the tradition and converts music into another medium which is more appropriate for her creativity. Interestingly enough, when Joe mourns for Dorcas, Violet wants to know more about the girl and her past. In this searching process, Violet's discovering of self with Dorcas consequently leads her to discover the real or the self. Yamini K. Murthy finds "Violet's relationship with Dorcas becomes an affirmation of love of one woman for another although Violet starts out with hatred in her heart."[14] This affirmation of love with others develops into an understanding of the self in Violet's relationship with Alice, Dorcas' aunt. Finally, Alice's rapport with Violet helps her to learn the real meaning of life.

Sociology has been an effort to create a method of historicai and political science in a form dependent on a pre-elaborated philosophical system that of evolutionistic positivism, against which sociology rejected but only partially. Vulgar evolutionism is at the root of sociology, sociology cannot know the dialectical principle with its passage from quantity to quality. In this context, Frederic Jameson converts the Freudian concept of repression into a political unconscious and argues that what is not said is repressed history. Terry Eagleton's approach to critical analysis is praiseworthy in connection with the proper understanding of Morrison's narrative output. Eagleton as well as Gramsci are right particularly in the context of *Paradise*. Eagleton redefines and reshapes "ideology in terms of all systems of representations (religion, aesthetics, apart from political theories) that reorient the individual's mental make-up through lived experiences. He emphasizes that it is the reworking of ideology's working on reality that produces the meanings and perceptions in the text."[15] In fact, 'literature is not fiction, a picture of the real because it cannot define itself simply as a figuration, and appearance of reality. By a complex process, literature is a production of certain reality. In this theoretical framework, Morrison's novels stand true to the letters and her *Paradise* (1998) becomes a key point of study and observation.

The more acute sense of black oppression in white America can be traced in Morrison's latest novel *Paradise* which recounts the triumphs and trials of the black community. The black Americans imaginatively remap their own world that is radically free from white hegemony. However, it becomes apparent that *Paradise* becomes a saga of suffering of blacks' physical and psychic wounds. *Paradise* deals with the story of all-black town of Ruby and the neighboring community of women who occupy the convent located just outside the Oklahoma town. The plot-setting of *Paradise* is tne mid-1970s Ruby, so close to the Black Arts Movements. Primarily, Ruby's stewardship rests in the hands of the Morgan twins, Deacon and Steward whose selection of past events and their interpretation of contemporary events help to stabilize their rule. *Paradise* illustrates a complementary inversion of white race chastity in which the pursuit of purity is employed as a means of sheltering oneself from white supremacy. The circumscription of women's freedom, sexuality and reproduction is maintained in the name of the community's self-defence which some men may address as paradise. It is not mere coincidence when Pat observes: "everything that worries them must come from women." Deacon also explains that "women always the key."

Morrison's narrative world offers a threadbare analysis of the social reality in which she was born and bred up. The subtle observation of the facts suggests that the contemporary sociological condition shapes the human psychology. Human psyche is always instrumental in every kind of action that flares up the creative imagination. Morrison, this way, becomes an epoch-making voice of the age on the level of psychological probing and proposition. Derrida might be locating the meaning only in the text and rejecting the fixity but in case of Morrison's novels it is justifiable to say that she records and reflects the inevitable social factors which determine the character of the human being as well as the society. No doubt, the debate over post-modernity stimulates a reappraisal of modernity as a socio-cultural phenomenon. Morrison's literary talk is the real inquiry of the actual socio-economic and political condition. She has a concept that invites a lot of responses on the nature and direction of present-day society, in a globalised context. The square view of Morrison's narrative art makes it suggestive that from her first creative venture to the last, she seems to be making an inquiry from realistic approach and at last she seems to be championing the causes of postmodernistic treatment of the facts and fictions. The present ongoing Presidential electioneering process in America establishes the black leader like Barack Obama in a strong position. In time to come he may emerge victorious by defeating his rival of the Republic party but it does not mean that racism and ethnicity of the American society have gone into oblivion or it has become a story of bygone age. "However, one should not mistake this extraordinary development for a sign that race and racism are disappearing from American social and political life."[16]

NOTES

1. David Lyon, *Postmodernity* (Second edition, Viva, 2002), 91
2. *Ibid.*, 97.
3. Qtd. Bernard W. Bell, *Afro-American Novel and Its Tradition* (Amherst: Massachusetts Press, 1977), 103.
4. Barbara Smith, "Doing Research on Black American Women," *Women Studies Newsletter*, 4 (Spring.1976)
5. Gloria Wade-Gayles, *No Crystal Stair: Visions of Race and Sex in Black Women's Fiction* (New York: The Pilgrim Press, 1984), 3-4.
6. Joel Kovel, *White Racism: A Psychohistory* (New York: Columbia UP, 1984), 18.
7. Beal Frances, "Double Jeopardy: To be Black and Female," *The Black Women: An Anthology* (New York: Signet, 1973), 90.
8. Jessica Harris, "Interview with Toni Morrison," *Essence*, 7, 8 (1976), 54.
9. Arunima Ray, "The Quest for 'Home' and 'Wholeness' in *Sula* and *Meridian*: Afro-American identity in Toni Morrison and Alice Walker," *Indian Journal of American Studies*, 23, 2 (Summer 1993), 61.
10. N. Krishnaswamy, John Varghese and Sunita Mishra, *Contemporary Literary Theory, A Student's Companion* (Macmillan, 2001), 57.
11. Angelo Bonnie, "The Pain of Being Black: An Interview," *Time*, 22 May 1989, 48.
12. Usha Shourie, "The Morrison Music: Narrative Style in *Jazz*," *Indian Journal of American Studies*, 23, 2 (Summer 1993), 68.
13. Doreatha Drummond Mbalia, "Women who Run with Wild: The Need for Sisterhood in *Jazz*," *Modern Fiction Studies*, 39, 3 and 4 (Fall/Winter, 1993), 635.
14. Yamini K. Murthy, "Gender Solidarity and Discovery of Self in Morrison's *Tar Baby* and *Jazz*," *Indian Journal of American Studies*, 82.
15. *Contemporary Literary Theory, A Student's Companion*, 102.
16. S. Shankar, "Post-Racial America?," *The Hindu, Sunday Magazine*, August 24, 2008, 5.

Racial Discourse in Toni Morrison's *The Bluest Eye*

A. HARIPRASANNA
S.V. University, Tirupati

> Racism is a man-made, man-enforced phenomenon . . . may be defined as all of the learned behaviour and learned emotions on the part of a grout of people towards another group whose physical characteristics are dissimilar to the formal group; behaviour and emotions that compel one group to conceive of and to treat the other on the basis of its physical characteristics alone, as if it did not belong to the human race.[1]

> The basic myth of racism is that white skin colour brings with it superiority that the white is more intelligent, more virtuous.[2]

Toni Morrison's *The Bluest Eye*, "a neo-slave narrative," is concerned with the theme of racial exploitation during the World War period. Owing to the then existing circumstances of sexism and racism, Pecola Breedlove becomes a victim of the white society. Marked early in heı life as ugly, she yearns for blue eyes, the ultimate standard of beauty as "white American prescription for beauty include blonde hair, white skin, and above all, blue eyes."[3]

The Bluest Eye, "a timeless study of a social outcast who rejects herself,"[4] implies an underlying desire for assimilation, verification and acceptance by white people. The novel revolves round the theme of slavery and racial oppression and its far-reaching consequences.

Living amongst a family that has been victimized by racial discrimination for ages, Pecola longs for blue eyes, praying ardently every night, so she could be accepted in the white society. Thrown into the blinding conviction that only a miracle could relieve her, she would never know her beauty. She would see only what there was to see: "the eyes of other people." (65) Themselves victims of slavery, Pauline and Cholly, by their behaviour help Pecola's mental degeneration. Obsessed with her own ugliness Pecola yearns to be blue-eyed and beautiful, hoping against hope that such beauty would fulfil her desire to be loved and needed for herself.

The tragedy in *The Bluest Eye* derives from two factors: the desire for blue eyes by a black girl, incongruous in itself but all the more so because it implies a desire for acceptance; and the frustration and impotence of a group of people whose daily prayer for survival is blended with a heavy desire for tolerance and freedom.[5]

Centering as it is around the tragic life of Pecola and her parents' failure to give her stability, the novel also explores the life the Black people lead—that of frustration and misery without neither thought nor regard for themselves: "No one could have convinced them that they were not relentlessly and aggressively ugly . . . you looked at them and wondered why they were so ugly; you looked closely and could not find the source. Then you realised that it came from conviction, their conviction."[6]

Pecola becomes the scapegoat of her parents and especially her mother's frustration and disappointment in life. Pecola's tragedy in life is closely linked with her mother's miserable circumstances. Pauline Breedlove fails as a mother and parent in her inability to bring her child up as a loved one: "to her love is a well-spring from which she would draw the most destructive emotions . . . seeking to imprison the beloved, curtailing freedom in every way." (95) Her dissatisfaction with life and the oppressive, racist society in general makes her no exemplary other. In fact it is she who is the major cause for Pecola's obsession with white standards of beauty and mental alienation: "She steals the life beyond rescue, beyond salvation."[7] A feeling of not being wanted and her inability to estimate her own worth leads to Pecola's personal disintegration. Ignored very much and blamed for she knows not what, Pecola lacks self-esteem. Disillusioned as they are with life, Pecola's parents do not know how to love;

and they cannot give their children a sense of self, for they have none of their own.[8]

Suffering rejection at the hands of her own mother, who acts rather like a glorified servant in a white household, Pecola withdraws more and more into her private world of suffering. Being a witness to the love and affection received by the Fisher's child—for which she has been longing—makes Pecola's withdrawal complete. Subjected as she is to that most dreaded condition of impoverished communities, being "out-doors," with no place to go and remaining an outsider, Pecola lives in a private world that is virtually untouched by change. Thus "The role that the African American community played in sealing Pecola's doom"[9] is not a negligible one. Claudia admits that it is so: "We were not free, merely licensed; we were not compassionate, we were polite; not good but well behaved. We substituted good grammar for rearranged lies and called it truth." (159)

Pauline Breedlove, Pecola's mother, is also a victim of notions that dictate that values and patterns of affluent culture should be imitated. Affected as she is by her own unhappy life as an adolescent and woman, in bondage both internally and externally, Pauline tries to escape her loneliness by conforming to the expectations of those she envies. Alienated from her own femininity in a racially dominated society, she denies the harsh reality of existence—the reality of her own life and family, but this time she substitutes for it not movies, but rather her cordial relationship with the Fishers, the white people for whom she works. Pauline loves the praise and luxury she enjoys in her employers' household, and because her home and family offer her no such perquisites:[10] "more and more she neglected her house, her children, her man—they were like the . . . dark edges that made the daily life with the Fishers lighter, more delicate, more lovely." (99)

By rejecting her own daughter, Pauline drives Pecola further into the shell and affirms Pecola's sense of ugliness and unworthiness: "[She] rejects her own daughter because she has erased from her psyche the line separating reality from illusion, mammyhood from motherhood."[11]

Pecola's sense of isolation and alienation is almost complete for "all she has learned about herself from school, from her peers and the world around her is that she is black, poor and ugly, the antithesis of all that society values."[12] The culprits in the crimes against Pecola, then, are not just the social conditions that destroyed first her parents and then Pecola herself, but also those within the black community who use the less fortunate to facilitate their own success in a racial society[13]:

> We were so beautiful when we stood astride her ugliness. Her simplicity decorated us, her guilt sanctified us, her pain made us glow with health, her awkwardness made us think we had a sense of humor. Her inarticulateness made us believe we were eloquent. Her poverty kept us generous . . . our eyes on her, padded our characters with her frailty, and yawned in the fantasy of our strength. (159)

Pecola's disturbing desire to know how "you get somebody to love you" (29) remains unfulfilled leading only to self-hatred and self-destruction. Cholly's own inadequacy, guilt, love and his helpless inability to do anything about it manifests itself in the physical violation of his daughter: "guilt, pity and then love. . . What could he do for her—even? . . . What give her? . . . What could a burnt-out black man say to the bunched bark of his eleven-year-old daughter?" (127)

Cholly is a poor role model for his daughter but in contrast to Pauline's obsession with order, Cholly's life is completely chaotic. Shattered by the way others have treated him, Cholly is ultimately unable to function as a member of human society: abandoned in a junk heap by his mother, rejected for a crap game by his father, there was nothing more to lose. "He was alone with his own perceptions and appetites, and they alone interested him." (126) Just as Pauline's life would have been improved by access to paints and crayons, the only solution to Cholly's dilemma, Morrison suggests, is to deal with his life artistically: "the pieces of Cholly's life could become coherent only in the head of a musician." (125) He violates her body as the others violated her spirit and pushes her into "final withdrawl"[14] which makes her disintegration complete.

Pecola's isolation and alienation is now total. She is victimized by both parents because they are made incapable of nurturing her by the limiting phenomena of race, sex, and class. Out of a deep well of self-hatred and psychic pain, they give Pecola the fullest measure of their misery. Pauline loves Pecola, but she beats her. Cholly loves Pecola, but rapes her.[15]

There is no hope of revival for Pecola. Even the marigolds planted by Claudia and others fail to bloom, signifying the utter hopelessness of the situation. Pecola never had a chance to survive in the hostile environment nor would she in future. As Claudia observes:

> the land of the entire country was hostile to marigolds that year. The soil is bad for certain kinds of flowers. Certain seeds it will not nurture, certain fruit it will not bear, and when the land kills of its own volition, we acquiesce and say the victim had no light to live. We are wrong of course, but it doesn't matter. It's too late. At least on the edge of my town, among the garbage and the sunflowers of my town, it's much, much, much too late. (160)

In order to give the Pecolas of this world a chance the blacks, her own group of people, "must first learn to love themselves."[16]

The Bluest Eye thus discusses a theme that is both universal and particular to the black female experience: the desire for freedom from racial and sexual victimization: the search for self-definition and autonomy, for personal spiritual wholeness, the search for equitable male-female relationships, the need for love and friendship.[17]

When asked about why she has written such a novel as this, Morrison replied: "I wrote *Sula* and *The Bluest Eye* because they were books I had wanted to read. No one had written them yet, so I wrote them."[18] She has shown clearly in Pecola that the needs of the women are basic human needs particular to the black community at a given point of time. It is admirable that she has given voice to the black women's experiences—in their search for a place in American society.[19]

NOTES

1. Calvin Hernton, *Sex and Racism in America* (New York: Grove, 1965), p. 175.
2. Kenneth Clark, *Black and White: The Ghetto Inside* (Lapides and Burrows, 1971), pp. 104-20.
3. Alphy J. Plakkoottam,"“Racial and Gender Discrimination in Fiction by Afro-American Women,” *Indian Journal of American Studies,* Vol. 20, No. 1, Winter 1990, pp. 17-18.
4. Melissa Walker, *Down from the Mountains Top* (New Haven: Yale University Press, 1991), p. 50.
5. Alphy J. Plakkoottam, p. 18.
6. Toni Morrison, *The Bluest Eye* (London: Chatto and Windus, 1979), p. 28.
7. Gloria Wade-Gayles, *No Crystal Stair: Visions of Race and Sex in Black Women's Fiction* (New York: Pilgrim Press), p. 67.
8. Jane S. Bakerman, “Failures of Love: Female Initiation in Novels of Toni Morrison,” *American Literature* (1981), p. 544.
9. Melissa Walker, p. 53.
10. Elizabeth B. House, “Artist and the Art of Living: Order and Disorder in Toni Morrison's Fiction,” *Modern Fiction Studies,* p. 32.
11. Wade-Gayles, p. 81.
12. Phyllis Klotman, “Dick-and-Jane and the Shirley Temple Sensibility in *The Bluest Eye,* ” *Black American Literature* (1979), p. 124.
13. Melissa Walker, p. 58.
14. Dorothy H. Lee, “The Quest for Self-Triumph and Failure in the Works of Toni Morrison,” in Harper and Stepto, p. 349.
15. Wade-Gayles, p. 77.
16. Claudia Tate, “Black Women Authors: An Emerging Voice,” *Topic,* No. 153, p. 160.
17. Judith H. Livingston, “Black Women's Lives, Black Women's Voices,” Feb. 1993, p. 33.
18. Claudia Tate, p. 60.
19. Judith H. Livingston, p. 34.

The Concept of Self: The Black Community in Toni Morrison's *The Bluest Eye*

NARAIN PRASAD SHUKLA

Wole Soyinka in his *Myth, Literature and the African World* talks in detail about the artist who builds a bridge over the abyss of chaos and destruction to bring the group across. Through this personal sacrifice, the group is brought to a higher plane of consciousness.[1] This is similar to Turner's state of "liminality" which is likened to "death, to being in the womb, to invisibility, to darkness, to bisexuality, to the wilderness, and to an eclipse of the sun or moon. Not only do individual artists brave this terrain, but many of the characters in the tradition of Black literature are also in states of "liminality." Ralph Ellison's *Invisible Man* is one example that comes readily to mind, as are many of Morrison's characters. But as Baker points out, this journey by the artist may not be appreciated by society, particularly if what the artist reveals about the identity of a people is not what society wants to hear. This is what the major problem has been for the Black woman writer. Black male writers have traditionally confronted White society, and revealed the conflicts that exist between Blacks and Whites. But the Black woman writer has traditionally written about what goes on within the Black community, and it is the exposure of this intimate life to the public that has evoked many harsh reactions. The Black woman writer is regarded as the individualist personified and therefore a witch.[3] But the Black woman writer has not stopped trying to understand her identity as well as the identity of her people. "To understand our origins we must journey through different straits and in the end we may only find confusion."[4] Toni Morrison has found a sense of order and has shown it clearly in her work. Morrison as a writer has made a significant contribution to American literature and the canon of writing by Black woman, her books contribute not only to the understanding of the specifics of life as a Black woman, but also the important issues of survival for the entire Black community. *The Bluest Eye* articulates Morrison's concern for the Black community, which then manifests itself in a concern for world in general. The novel is about the victimization of one small Black girl named Pecola. Self-hate makes her vulnerable to abuse not only from her family but from the entire community as well. Pecola is obsessed with the myth of physical beauty and as a result is plunged into a world of madness. Her life is devoid of love and is full of brutality and ugliness. Nature reflects the stunted growth of this child as the marigolds refuse to grow in her town. Pecola is totally defenceless as she has no sense of self, because that is something which can only be obtained if one is first nurtured and loved. Morrison contrasts Pecola's life to the normal pain of growing up for a Black girl like Claudia, to show how unprepared Pecola will be for the realities of adulthood.

The Bluest Eye is told by a narrator who is still a child. It is the world as seen through the eyes of a Black girl named Claudia who has a constant companion and friend in her sister Frieda. Theirs is an "ideal" nuclear family[5] and they live with their mother and father in a green house. Their house is cold and dark and is inhabited by roaches and mice. Claudia remembers the pain, anger, and humiliation that surrounded illness in this house, but with the passage of time she is able to put her experiences there into perspective:

> But was it really like that? As painful as I remember? Only mildly. Or rather, it was productive and fructifying pain, Love, thick and dark as Alga syrup, eased up into the cracked window. I could smell it—taste it—sweet, musty, with an edge of wintergreen in its base—everywhere in that house.[6]

Claudia remembers the smells, touch, taste and, above all, the ubiquitous love of her family and her house, where adults battled to keep the children alive. Life is tied with pain from birth, and when pain is no longer felt, death is near. Old Black women illustrate this point. "They were old enough to be irritable when and where they chose, tired enough to look forward to death, disinterested enough to accept the idea of pain while ignoring the presence of pain. They were, in fact and at last, free." (110) Pain, a part of life, can be either destructive or productive; there was a response for it, and because of it she was able to stay alive and grow to adulthood.

In the novels of Morrison, the Black people believe themselves to be ugly. In *The Bluest Eye,* Pecola Breedlove is told the day she is born that she is ugly. She lives with her brother Sammy, her mother Pauline, and her father Cholly. Though their surname is Breedlove, ironically enough, all they breed is self-hate and mutual destruction. They all believe themselves to be ugly, and as a result, ugliness becomes all-pervasive in their home and in their countenances:

> It was as though some mysterious all-knowing master had said, "You are ugly people." They had looked about themselves and saw nothing to contradict the statement; saw, in fact, support for it leaping at them from every billboard, every movie, every glance. . . . And they took the ugliness in their hands, threw it as a mantle over them, and went about the world with it. (34)

Morrison's tone sounds almost Biblical when she describes the decree given to Breedlove and symbolically, all Blacks—that Black will be ugly and White will be beautiful. The Breedloves are an extreme because they have not questioned whether this commandment has been given to them by God or the Devil. Pauline accepts as her standard of beauty what she has absorbed from Hollywood images. However, because she believes herself to be ugly—she is physically unable to attain these Hollywood standards—her children are taught that they are ugly too.

Pecola considers herself to be so ugly that her only concept of self is in terms of a white girl named Shirley Temple. She consumes enormous quantities of milk so that she can hold the cup and gaze the image of Shirley Temple in it. She even eats

Mary Jane candies because she believes that by ingesting them she has somehow ingested beauty. "To eat candy is somehow to eat the eyes, eat Mary Jane. Love Mary Jane." (43) Pecola is obsessed with blue eyes. She is able to suppress all her senses and emotions, she is able to hide behind ugliness, but she is not able to keep from seeing the ugliness that surrounds her in her home. Her home is filled with violence and obscenity. She wants to disappear, to leave and be free of the physical sickness she feels and the horrors she witnesses. So she prays for a miracle: "Please God," she whispered into the palm of her hand, "please make me disappear." (39) She finds that with extreme concentration she is able to make all the parts of her body fade except her eyes. "Almost done, almost. Only her tight, tight eyes were left. They were always left." (15) There can be no miracle for Pecola in the real world, and being a child, she can only translate the activities around her in terms of herself. She therefore feels that she is somehow to blame for the brutality and violence that surround her. Her eyes transmit ugliness to her mind and implant it on her consciousness. Since they perceive ugliness they must in turn be ugly, and if they were beautiful, blue, then they would only see beauty. It would also hold true that if she were beautiful, people would treat her in a beautiful manner. To Pecola, beauty is being seen and acknowledged as a human being.

The concept of self of Black people revolves round an idea of "freedom" that Black men have but which Black women do not possess. Thus, Sammy can run away from the family but Pecola must stay and somehow cope with the situation. However free Black males may be, they don't automatically have healthier psyches. Cholly had been abandoned at the age of four days and orphaned at thirteen. His life, up to the time that he meets Pauline, is a series of broken ties with people and society until he reaches the point where all his energies are directed at satisfying his own appetites and desires:

> He was free to live his fantasies, and free even to die, the how and when of which held no interest to him. In those days, Cholly was truly free. Abandoned in a junk heap by his mother, rejected for a crap game by his father, there was noting more to lose. (125-26)

Cholly is free and dangerous because he has no restraints, obligations, or parameters for behaviour and emotion. The only truly free people are the old Black women who have "carried a world on their heads. (110) Their freedom is their reward for having survived life, for having carried its burdens, and not abandoned responsibilities and relationships. It seems that man cannot, should not, be totally free, because he then becomes absorbed in self-stimulation and gratification which can be harmful to those around him. A free man also uses the self as the absolute standard for his behaviour; and man, being human, cannot by himself decipher all the lines between right and wrong, good and evil. This is why incest, in Cholly's mind, is not destructive or unnatural.

Cholly is a man who has experienced the world; while Pauline, on the other hand, has been sheltered, experiencing very little in her life. The tragedy of their union is that it kills their imagination, because they are never able to mature into real adulthood. Without imagination, they can never express their experiences and feelings, and therefore they seek heavens where they do not have to think and feel—Cholly finds refuge in the bottle and Pauline in being a servant. Both refuges are fantasy worlds. Yet, if Cholly had learned music and Pauline painting, they would not have had to focus their lives on dreams and fantasy. Cholly could have made sense of why he was abandoned by his mother, rejected by his father, orphaned by Aunt Jimmy and unable to communicate with old Blue Jack. Cholly was named after a dead uncle and never knew his father. He goes in search of his fantasy father who has never shown any interest in him at all. When he finally finds him, the rejection is complete and absolute, and the old Cholly is destroyed. He pales, soils himself, and runs away from all human contact. Cholly must be reborn if he is to continue to live, but this time he is self-made and delivered. He misses the love and affection of his Aunt Jimmy, the nourishment she gave him; instead he must settle for lemonade and the attention of three prostitutes. "They gave him back his manhood; which he takes aimlessly." (125) He is reborn in the flesh and is a free man.

Whereas Cholly has had many experiences and is free, Pauline is sheltered and had led an isolated existence from outside stimulation, except for the four brief years at school. At fifteen, Pauline begins to awaken to her fast approaching womanhood. Her life is ordered and she is happy to stay at home keeping the house while her mother works. Pauline expects things to happen to her; she expects that she will be found by a perfect stranger, sexually gratified, loved, and led by the hand to the promised land. When a stranger does appear in the form of Cholly, she lets him take her hand and lead her out of Kentucky, away from the cocoon of her family, to Ohio, the Promised Land.

When Cholly and Pauline arrive in Ohio, they find life quite suffocating. Pauline tries to understand why she is an outsider, why she cannot make friends, and she decides that it is because she looks different from Northern women. Material things—make-up, hair-style, clothes—are her key to enter into the community. "The sad thing was that Pauline did not really care for clothes and make-up. She merely wanted other women to cast favourable glances her way." (94) Pauline is like a small child who needs to be approved of and stimulated, but the worst is that she never grows up to be able to do these things for herself. Money, clothes and make-up are simplistic solutions to the complex problems; nonetheless, that is how Pauline seeks to resolve them. She tries to get a job, but instead of answers she only finds new problems. She and Cholly argue now because he does not like the way she spends her money. Her life becomes ritualistic—she goes to work every morning and comes home to argue with Cholly every night.

The employment most readily available to Pauline is domestic work.[7] This is the first time she has ever had any intimate contact with Whites. She finds her White employer to be "simple-minded." She cannot understand why this White family is not happy, given all the money and comfort they possess: "You'd think with a pretty house like that and all the money they could hold on to, they would enjoy one another. She haul off and cry over the leastest thing." (94) It is ironic that Pauline should have this observation, because she and Cholly are also in much better financial situation at this point, and they too are getting along terribly. Pauline finds the White family to be sloppy and dirty, and every time she is at the point where she could begin to like her employer, the White woman interferes with Pauline's work as if she knows more about cleanliness.

Pauline's situation is difficult but not untypical of Black women who have to do domestic work. She is able to do her job and handle the situation until the White woman asks her to make a choice between her and Cholly. In Pauline's mind, there is no basis for making such a choice—there are no loyalties, no favours. In fact, it is insulting for Pauline even to hear such a request: "She said she would let me stay if I left him. I thought about that. But later on it didn't seem none too bright for a Black woman to leave a Black man for a white woman." (95) The White woman feels insulted when Pauline chooses to stay with her man, and uses this as an excuse to cheat her out of her hard-earned wages. Pauline still has rainbows and laughter in her mind, despite the tensions of her marriage; her life is incomprehensible to the White woman. Pauline decides it is just her employer's inability to understand rainbows and laughter that makes her preach the roles of men and women, while saying that how she is looking out for Pauline's future. To her, Cholly is beautiful and White features are unappealing. She rejects the impracticality and undesirability of White norms for her Black lifestyle when she is faced with them in the flesh, yet when they are put before her on the silver screen, she swallows them hook, line, and sinker.

Morrison found Black woman the corner-stone of the community: they are an "umbrella figure, culture bearer, in community with not just her children but all children"[8] In *The Bluest Eye,* this role of woman is given to Pauline who feels that she has responsibilities as wife, mother, and provider. The demands of her life force her to put dreams aside. She instinctively reorders her world in terms that make sense to her.

> When Sammy and Pecola were still young, Pauline had to go back to work. She was older now with no time for dreams and movies. It was time to put all the pieces together, make coherence where before there had been none. (100)

Pauline becomes an adult in her responsibilities but she does have an adult's ability to sort out and assimilate complex information; to put things into a proper perspective. The more simply things can be explained and justified, despite their complexity, the better she likes it. Ironically, Pauline begins to fit better into the community. Because she works and goes to church, she suddenly has access to the fellowship of other women.

> She came into her own with the women who had despised her, by being more moral than they; she avenged herself on Cholly by forcing him to indulge in the weaknesses she despised. Holding Cholly as a model of sin and failure, she bore him like a crown of thorns, and her children like a cross. (100)

Pauline is not the backbone of her family, providing support and encouragement to her husband and love and nurture to her children. She is not the cross but the martyr, who lives only to die for a holy cause. Cholly, in his weakness and sin, is the perfect foil to her holiness and perfection; however, his reformation would have been devastating to her because she only feels perfect in contrast to him. Pauline becomes a reflection of the powerful images that surround her—ugly in contrast to white women, and good in contrast to evil black men. These are her excuses for not making herself a whole, beautiful Black woman. She does not spare her children from her exaggerated sacrifice of herself in a false martyrdom, for she assumes they are as evil as their father and as ugly as she is. She uses fear and violence to shape and control her children. Pauline thus ensures that Sammy will grow up to be like his father and Pecola like her. Sammy and Pecola are thus even more defenceless to fight the powerful images that seek to enslave their minds.

The characters thus far discussed are part of a Black community which Morrison paints as the background in this novel. This community has its own standards of right and wrong, beauty and ugliness, and its own methods of healing wounds. Claudia and Frieda's family life reflects many of the norms of the larger community, while the Breedloves reflect all that can go wrong. Cholly is an abnormal character, incomprehensible to the Black community, who cannot understand why he puts his family "outdoors":

> There is a difference in being put *out* and being put *outdoors*. If you are put out, you go somewhere else; if you are outdoors, there is no place to go. The distinction is subtle but final. (18)

When Cholly turns his family out of their apartment through his meanness and carelessness, they are left outdoors because they have no friends, family, or support network to rely on; they may turn instead to the social welfare system to provide them with shelter. The state of being "outdoors" highlights to the Black their powerlessness in the social system. A need to own material things, tangible signs that one does exist becomes a drive in community. Cholly and Breedloves are outside of the community drives and norms: they have always been "outdoors." Some of the men of the community who have the drive to possess and own property seek spouses who will help them build their nests, as for the women, some of them will be wives—and then there are the "brown girls." These brown girls will become brown women, mothers, wives who will adopt the White norm of respectability. It is a norm that has been adopted by a part of the Black community which has moulded their daughters in its image. What they do not realize is that it is an image that has been created to suppress and destroy the life of the Black community.

Not only is Morrison critical of Black women who imbue themselves with white propaganda and poison the community with it, she is also critical of those Black men who do not fulfil their roles as men but instead prey upon the community. One of these men is Henry Washington, a boarder in the home of Claudia and Frieda. Claudia's mother describes him positively in a conversation with one of her friends: "He's just sensible. A steady worker with quiet ways." (67) These women remark upon the fact that he is not married, blaming it on the lack of "desirable" Black women in the community. They do not consider that he may have some strange idiosyncrasy that would make him undesirable to any of them. Ironically, the same standards of respectability are applied to Pauline as to Henry—the ability to work hard and steadily for Whites—while in actuality both are brutalizing the children of the community. Washington, a "sensible quiet man" who reads pornographic magazines, patronizes prostitutes, and tries to molest Frieda.

It is important to include some mention of magic in the lives of the Black people, for this is a force that works both ways, a force that can heal or hurt, a force that can be used for good as well as for evil. Magic is the seeking of power by the powerless. Henry Washington uses magic to entertain Claudia and Frieda, hoping to gain their friendship and their parents' trust; Claudia and Frieda resort to it in their effort to help Pecola and her unborn child. As for Pecola, she seeks a miracle to free her from the nightmare of her existence. She goes to Soaphead, the Interpreter of 'Dreams,' to ask him to give her blue eyes. At first, he claims that he is unable to help her because he is not a magician or a miracle worker, but her need and her belief resist; he continues a ritual to make her believe that the impossible has happened. Pecola thus finds solace in miracles and magic.

The power of magic is to be seen in the context of the adult conversation in which Pecola is blamed for her rape and the unborn child is wished dead. Claudia and Frieda feel an instinctive compassion and love for Pecola and the child. Thus, faced with a reality that needs to be changed and needing additional power to affect this change, they find magic the only course open to them. Claudia and Frieda's magic is well intentioned, a healing force, a magic that works with and for life, a magic allied with life and Nature. Their use of magic goes hand-in-hand with their love and compassion for Pecola. Thus, they plant seeds and sing magical words over them to help them grow, believing that just as they would sprout and grow, so too would Pecola's baby.

This ritual is in stark contrast to the one which Pecola performs, giving an old dog some poisoned meat and perceiving his reactions to being a sign that blue eyes will be bestowed upon her. This sign that is given to Pecola is one contrived by Soaphead and it is clearly non-life magic, contrary to Nature, in conflict with the cosmic life force that heals and makes things grow, but in Pecola's mind the miracle takes effect. The situation of the Breedlove family is such an abomination to the community, and to Nature itself that inevitably the infant dies and Pecola goes insane. No marigolds blossom in the town that year. Claudia and Frieda's seeds never grow, because the soil is sterile, contaminated and mere magic cannot render it fertile again.

Morrison's goal pursued via fiction laden with ritual and myth is to restore a sense of wholeness to her people. The various characters in *The Bluest Eye* participate in many rituals, each of which serves as a special function. One example of a naming ritual is the way Cholly's family waited, not naming him until the ninth day of his life, as a sign that he would be staying in this realm for a while. Another important ritual that can be found in any Black community is a funeral; and in *The Bluest Eye,* it is the funeral of Aunt Jimmy. The funeral is divided into different pans, each one representing a facet of community's world-view, and showing how readily people adapt to the roles that life and death impose upon their lives:

> The funeral banquet was a peal of joy after the thunderous beauty of the funeral. There was grief over the waste of life, the stunned wonder at the ways of God, and the restoration of order in nature at the graveyard. (113)

The Black community holds God and His ways in reverence, not challenging or questioning His will. The funeral is a ritual of catharsis as ancient as man. It takes them collectively to the brink of the unknown, death, where each individual is expected to express grief and fear. Then, on returning from the cemetery, they join together once more to celebrate their own liveliness, which demands to be fed with food and laughter. This return to life is epitomized by Darlene who gently brings Cholly out of mourning, and back from his encounter with death, by participating in the ultimate celebration of life, and for his initiation into manhood. Morrison also effectively embodies the philosophy of reverence for life; she knows that life and death are two sides of the same coin, and thus she never tries to change or recreate life, but simply accepts.

Throughout the novel, Pecola is used as a dumping ground by most of the other characters. She is not considered a witch; rather, she is the scapegoat, the sacrificial victim. Cholly, Soaphead and the boys in the schoolyard, for instance, with their battered egos and tortured psyches, can safely vent their rage and frustration on her because she has no defence system, and thus cannot fight back. She is a rarity of Nature—a completely defenceless creature—and when she can no longer stand the ugliness and pain which her eyes reveal to her, there is no recourse for her but to withdraw into her sanctuary of blue eyes and madness, where she can no longer be hurt. She flutters around aimlessly, looking like a bird that is trying to fly away into the blue of the sky, trying in vain to be free of this earth, cannot because it is crippled:

> The birdlike gestures are worn away to a mere picking and plucking her way between the tire rims and the sunflowers, between coke bottles and milkweed, among all the waste and beauty of the world which is what she herself was. (159).

But, of course, Pecola cannot fly away to the heavens. Instead, she remains earthbound, scratching the ground with sightless eyes, a constant reminder to the community of its collective guilt. The ethos of the Black community does not, condone such self-abuse by one of its members; and because of the guilt they feel for not helping Pecola sooner, or indeed at all, their contempt for her is intensified. In their eyes, she represents all of the possible horrors of being Black and female in America. She is allowed to stay in the community, but she is relegated to a spot amongst the insane, who are tolerated but ignored as they are harmless.

In *The Bluest Eye,* Morrison gathers together an assortment of elements—ritual, myth and complexities—of human relationships and weaves them into the framework of Nature to create a novel rich in natural imagery. The events of the story follow the cycle of the seasons: in winter, the childhood and innocence reign supreme; in spring, there is flowering and maturation; in summer, adulthood, work and love abound; and in autumn, there is old age, death and freedom. This is a sensual world where men—like dogs—want to smell the "funk" of life, and where women work and suffer like mute horses. It is a world where children use their senses to decipher the mysteries of Nature. It is by having their senses stimulated that children are able to learn and grow, with self-knowledge being the ultimate goal. But the final, most important lesson in growing up is the refinement of one's sense of perception, for without this skill, mere awareness can only provide an overabundance of useless sensual information, and without lucid conception to give meaning and order to the information provided by one's senses, further growth is impossible. There must be no more Pecolas thrown into unyielding and infertile soil to die before they have a chance to live.

NOTES

1. Wole Soyinka, *Myth, Literature and the African World* (Cambridge: Cambridge University Press, 1976), pp. 150-55.
2. Victor Turner, *The Ritual Process* (Harmondsworth: Penguin, 1969), p. 81.
3. Houston Baker, *The Journey Back* (Chicago: University of Chicago Press, 1980), p. 117.
4. *Ibid.*, p. 1.
5. Gutman's studies of black families up to the twentieth century show that stable nuclear families were the norm prior to the great northern urban migrations of the twentieth century. See Herbert Gutman, *The Black Family in Slavery and Freedom, 1870-1925* (New York: Pantheon Books, 1976), pp. xviii-xxiv.
6. Toni *Morrison, The Bluest Eye* (N.Y.: Pocket Books, 1970), p. 14.
7. Joyce Ladner and Filomina Steady point out that the African woman was accustomed to working and being independent. Joyce Ladner, *Tomorrow's Tomorrow* (New York: Doubleday, 1971) pp. 18-24; Filomina Steady, *The Black Woman Cross-Culturally* (Cambridge, Massachusetts: Schenkman, 1981), pp. 22-34.
8. Robert Stepto, "Intimate Things in Place: A Conversation with Toni Morrison," *Chant of Saints,* ed. Michael Harper and Robert Stepto (Urbana, Illinois: University of Illinois Press, 1979), p. 228.

The Terrain of Race, Class and Gender in *The Bluest Eye*

BHARATI A. PARIKH
M.S. University, Baroda

Since the award of Nobel Prize to Toni Morrison for Literature in September 1993, the Euro-centric tradition has acknowledged a much awaited worthy claim. Morrison has created a breathtaking world of African American characters. They are visible minority in the white land. When she was asked about *The Bluest Eye* in an interview, she replied that she wanted to read such a book. As no one had ever written that kind of a novel, she wrote it.

The Bluest Eye can be considered as an epitome in literature as it depicts the life of poor, young, sensitive, neglected Pecola Breedlove. She belongs to the family of Breedlove where love is non-existent. White American literature had several black characters, but they are not the subject. They are made an object. In *Huckleberry Finn* Jim is as important as Huck, but who is at the centrestage? Huck only, from a white man's point of view. Hence Morrison creates her universe where black men and women, children and adults inhabit the fictional world.

The utter poverty of Cholly Breedlove brings in its trail miserable condition of being "put outdoors." Claudia as the narrator of the story, knows the societal condition of blacks, as she narrates in the "Autumn" part of the novel: "Being a minority in both caste and class, we moved about anyway on the hem of life, struggling to consolidate our weaknesses and hang on, or to creep singly up into the major folds of the garment." (18)

Thus the existence of the blacks is just on the periphery in society. The poverty is heart-rending. The one time happy, enchanted life of Pauline Breedlove, Cholly's wife, cracks like a mirror. She knows that she will never attain the early bliss, or experience the "rainbow feeling" in her poverty-stricken store front home which she had, initially, when she met and married Cholly. Hence she concentrates her attention, and an impulse for artistic outlet and order, on the white household where she works as a maid.

The issue of race and class is interrelated. Especially so in the case of poor black people. The assault on their self-respect is so deep that poverty is the shunned thing. Nine-year old Claudia knows how horrible it is to be "put outdoors." By and large, Claudia and Frieda were prepared to accept Pecola as their mother had informed them that a "case" was coming—a girl who had no place to go. "The county had placed her in our house for a few days until they could decide what to do, or, more precisely, until the family was reunited." (17)

The family or the definition of happy family is given at the outset in the novel. This is again a parody of the white values. The white family has a precise definition of a beautiful green and white painted house with a red door. In their lives, a family consists of a mother, a father, a son and a daughter. They possess a dog and a cat as well. The daughter Jane wants to play. She, one by one, goes to the father, mother, brother, dog and the cat. In turn none welcomes her or is prepared to play with her. This is the story of the fragmented family where the daughter Pecola who is very black, so ugly, is met with such cold attitude that she lapses into madness.

The poverty and helplessness turns Cholly Breedlove into an animal. "He had joined the animals; was, indeed, an old dog, a snake, a ratty nigger." These epithets suffice to let the readers know Cholly's humiliation, his reduced state from a man to an old dog. The anger experienced by the novelist is well brought out on the surface. The black men were not regarded as the members of the society, who had a right to have a job and a home. The poverty and the fear of being put outdoors led many a black family to breed in them "a hunger for property, for ownership."

Again there is a distinction of class within the blacks:

> Propertied black people spent all their energies, all their love, on their nests . . . they painted, picked, and poked at every corner of their houses. And these houses loomed like hothouse sunflowers among the rows of weeds that were the rented houses. (18)

Cholly Breedlove and his family belonged to the rented class. How did these people look upon the propertied class? The novelist is overt in expressing their position: "they cast furtive glances at these owned yards and porches." The tragic mode of Cholly's life is so pathetic as his family has been put outdoors, and he "had catapulted himself beyond the reaches of human consideration" (18). Thus, the issue of race and class is at the centrestage in *The Bluest Eye*. Morrison has scathingly parodied the concept of a happy and pretty house in the title of the new chapter where the letters are printed together without spacing, jumbling them like this:

> hereisthehouseitisgreenandwhiteithasareddooritisveryprettyitisvery prettyprettypretty

Thus, the novelist repeats the adverb "pretty" thrice, to highlight the "abandoned store front" house on the southeast corner of Broadway and Thirty-Fifth Street in Lorain, Ohio.

The life lived by Breedloves in the storefront brings out the pathos:

> They slipped in and out of the box of peeling gray, making no stir in the neighborhood, no sound in the labor force, and no wave in the mayor's office. Each member of the family in his own cell of consciousness, each making his own patchwork quilt of reality—collecting fragments of experience here, pieces of information there. (31)

Thus, the theme of class, in case of this poor Breedlove family is so crucial, that they neither have the wherewithal nor self-respect to sustain themselves in society. Poor Blacks are thus, not only poor but also looked down upon by all and one.

Pecola experiences total neglect on the part of white Sundries Store owner Yacobowski. He sells candies, fresh veg. and meat. Pecola, in order to buy Mary Jane brand of candies goes there. His response to Pecola's presence is described scathingly thus:

> Somewhere between retina and object, between vision and view, his eyes draw back, hesitate and hover. At some fixed point in time and space he senses that he need not waste the effort of a glance. (42)

Pecola tries hard to find out the root cause of such an attitude. Pecola could read the white man's racist attitude. As Pecola looks up at Yacobowski, she "sees the vacuum where curiosity ought to lodge. . . . The total absence of human recognition—the glazed separateness." (42) Pecola wonders at the cold attitude and surmises that it is perhaps due to his being a "grown" or a man, and she a little girl. The little girl Pecola, eager to be loved, adored and appreciated does not interest a white immigrant storekeeper whose "sensibilities have been blunted by a permanent awareness of loss." (42)

Pecola's experience of white male eyes is depicted sensitively, even accurately. Morrison, in creating Pecola, has voiced the inner feelings of many black girls and their dreary situation in life:

> She has seen interest, disgust, even anger in grown male eyes. Yet this vacuum is not new to her. It has an edge; somewhere in the bottom lid is the distaste. She has seen it lurking in the eyes of all white people. So, the distaste must be for her, her blackness. (42)

The Breedlove family believed that they were ugly. The concept of physical beauty prevalent in the white society told them so. They saw about themselves and saw nothing to contradict the statement, "You are ugly people." In fact all around them, they could read from "every billboard, every movie, every glance." In addition, the poverty stricken family "took the ugliness in their hands, threw it as a mantle over them, and went about the world with it." (34)

Pecola's ugliness is further derided by a sophisticated black woman, Geraldine, who learnt sophistication and pompous show of her home. Her only son Junior was strictly asked not to mix with black children though he longed to play with the black boys. His mother had explained to him the difference between coloured people and niggers:

> Colored people were neat and quiet; niggers were dirty and loud. He belonged to the former group: . . . his hair was cut as close to his scalp as possible to avoid any suggestion of wool, the part was etched into his hair by the barber. . . . The line between colored and nigger was not always clear; subtle and telltale signs threatened to erode it, and the watch had to be constant. (71)

In such a home, by chance Pecola enters, and meets an insulting "get out" from Geraldine. Thus, instead of support, one black woman hates a young girl who is derided by white store-owner, as well as the same community. This reveals the subtle class system within the black society. Geraldine is the one privileged well-to-do black.

The cause of catastrophe in the life of young black women is due to the misleading concept of beauty. Pauline in her moments of loneliness, when she leaves South and goes to North with Cholly, goes to movies. There, along with "the idea of romantic love, she was introduced to another—physical beauty." Morrison relates the havoc this idea creates in Pauline and Pecola's life:

> Probably the most destructive ideas in the history of human thought. Both originated in envy, thrived in insecurity, and ended in disillusion. In equating physical beauty with virtue, she stripped her mind, bound it, and collected self-contempt by the heap. (97)

Morrison's authorial comment says a lot in least words on the concept of beauty. A female in one culture may be considered beautiful on the basis of blue eyes, blonde hair and rosy cheeks. When this white people's concept of beauty among women is transferred without taking enough care to coloured people and their culture, the resultant tragedy is almost unbearable, choking. Morrison considers this as "probably the most destructive ideas in the history of human thought." (97)

Pauline's happiness with Cholly, and her life as a black woman who is working as a maid with a white family assume two totally different, separate existences. There is a gradual downfall in the family life in Breedlove home. The racial politics operates at several levels. One such outlet is found in silver screen:

> She [Pauline] was never able, after her education in the movies, to look at a face and not assign it some category in the scale of absolute beauty, and the scale was one she absorbed in full from the silver screen. (97)

Gradually, she neglected herself, her household, her children. When Pecola was born, she said to herself that "*I'd love it no matter what it looked like*." (98) In spite of her determination the wrong notion of beauty did not allow her to enjoy and love her daughter. Her inner thoughts and talk are rendered in italics in the novel. Finally, she cannot stand firm on her resolution. She surmises about Pecola: "A right smart baby she was. . . . Head full of pretty hair, but Lord she was ugly" (100).

She suffers from lack of amenities in her own house, whereas she enjoys unprecedental privileges in the Fishers' home. There she "found beauty, order, cleanliness, and praise." (101). The annihilation of self-image wrecks her happy family life: "as a model of sin and failure, she bore him [Cholly] like a crown of thorns, and her children like a cross" (100).

The racial, class and gender politics work so subtly that without realizing the dangers, Pauline succumbs to the lures of tantalizing white household and their way of life. Her life becomes compartmentalized. She kept the "order," and the "beauty," "the power, praise and luxury" of the Fishers "for herself, a private world, and never introduced it into her storefront, or to her children" (101-2):

> Then she bent toward respectability, and in so doing taught them fear: fear of being clumsy, fear of being like their father, fear of not being loved by God, fear of madness like Cholly's mother's. Into her son she beat a loud desire to run away, and into her daughter she beat a fear of growing up, fear of other people, fear of life. (102)

Thus, Pauline is doubly oppressed: being a black and being a woman. As Morrison talks to Tate that there is "a special kind of domestic perception that has its own violence . . . not bloody violence, but violence nonetheless (Tate, 23).

The repercussions are such that the troubled, quarrelsome life of Pauline and Cholly drive young Pecola to madness. But before she lapses into insanity she falls prey to fantasy. She tries to overcome the unbearable and harsh existence of day-to-day life of bickerings by her parents by praying for the prettiest, bluest eyes. She feels that just by looking at her pretty blue eyes, everything will be changed in her small household. Her parents will look at her pretty blue eyes and stop quarrelling.

The survival technique she resorts to is dangerous, but she fails to realize the danger inherent in it. It is not her naivety nor innocence, but victimization in the throes of class, race and gender politics.

Morrison expresses the genesis of her using the primer story, with its picture of a happy family. It is a "frame acknowledging the outer civilization." She further adds:

> The primer with white children was the way life was presented to the black people. As the novel proceeded I wanted that primer version broken up and confused, which explains that typographical running together of the words." (Le Clair, 29).

The visual images are a very important component of Morrison's 'narratives'. Morrison highlights this:

> The interest in vision, in seeing is a fact of black life. As slaves and ex-slaves, black people were manageable and findable, as no other slave society would be, because they were black. So there is an enormous impact from the simple division of color—more than sex, age or anything else. The complaint is not being seen for what one is. (*Ibid.*)

Thus, Morrison justifies the reason for her hatred of white people, and their hatred for black people "is not."

It is not easy to transform the whites' way of thinking. The white race has enjoyed the sense of being superior as a class and race for over more than three centuries.

For Pecola Breedlove, to look beautiful, to overcome the ugliness of physical reality is the uppermost, in her dream and waking thought. This takes her to an Anglophile Soaphead Church, who becomes a "Reader, Adviser, and Interpreter of Dreams" in Lorain. Due to lack of courage "to confront homosexuality," this cinnamon-eyed West Indian limited his interests to little girls. He played God and performed a very good show. He "caused a miracle" for Pecola who went to this freak, Soaphead Church asking: "I'd like a pair of new blue eyes." So he gave her the eyes. These eyes are visible to none but Pecola. Thus, Pecola, after the assault by Cholly Breedlove on his eleven year daughter, lapses into fantasy. She then roams about the garbage heap on the outskirts of Lorain.

Pecola is the one character for whom none in the white or the black neighborhood shows concern, worry, care, anxiety or pity. Though Claudia and Frieda are worried about Pecola's baby, they hear elders talking that the baby won't survive. In their innocence and desire to defy the love of white baby dolls, Shirley Temples and Maureen Peals, they felt a strong need for someone to want the black baby to live. But their efforts go in vain. Claudia's thoughts render their position clearly:

> We had defended ourselves since memory against everything and everybody, considered all speech a code to be broken by us, and all gestures subject to careful analysis; we had become headstrong, devious and arrogant. Nobody paid us any attention, so we paid very good attention to ourselves. Our limitations were not known to us—not then. (149).

This reveals young black girl's helplessness to change the life, the tragic situation of their friend Pecola Breedlove.

They plant the marigold seeds, too deep into the soil. Utter incantationary magic words so that the seeds will sprout. Frieda and Claudia were disappointed, as the marigold seeds did not sprout. The baby was born, but died soon. Pecola went mad:

> A little black girl yearns for the blue eyes of a little white girl, and the horror at the heart of her yearning is exceeded only by the evil of fulfillment. (158)

The destruction is so total, that even the nine and ten year old Claudia and Frieda could not face her. Pecola is reduced to a picture of gloom and despondency:

> she spent her days, her tendril, sap-green days, walking up and down, up and down, her head jerking to the beat of a drummer so distant only she could hear. Elbows bent, hands on shoulders, she flailed her arms like a bird in an eternal, grotesquely futile effort to fly. Beating the air, a winged but grounded bird, intent on the blue void it could not reach—could not even see—but which filled the valleys of the mind. (158)

Thus, we feel the exhortations of black existence in white America. Claudia Tate tellingly expresses the complexities of race and gender in the Introduction to *Black Women Writers at Work:* "Nowhere else in America is the social terrain more complex, controversial and contradictory than where a racial minority and the 'weaker' gender intersect." (xv)

Black women artists like Toni Morrison and Maya Angelou, Alice Walker and Gloria Naylor are in the forefront in charting the territory so far uncharted. By virtue of their race and gender, black women writers find themselves at two points of intersection: "One where Western culture cuts across vestiges of African heritage, and one where male-female attitudes are either harmoniously parallel, subtly divergent, or in violent collision." (Tate xvi) All the characters in Morrison's novels are engaged in "perplexing struggles to maintain their human dignity and emotional sensitivity in an *impersonal*, *alien*, and frequently threatening world." (*Ibid.*)

In almost all black women writers we discern, what it means to be human, a condition not entirely determined by genetic make-up but also comprising conscious volition. Both Morrison and Walker, being black and female, write from unique vantage point. They project their vision of the world, society, community, family, their lovers, even themselves, most often through the eyes of black female characters and poetic personae. Their angle of vision allows them to see what white people especially males, seldom see: "with one penetrating glance they cut through layers of institutionalized racism and sexism and uncover a core of social contradictions and intimate dilemmas which plague all of us, regardless of our race or gender. Through their art they share their vision of possible resolution with those who cannot see." (Tate xvi)

Works Cited

Toni Morrison, *The Bluest Eye.* New York: Holt, 1970.

Thomas Le Clair, "The Language Must not Sweat," A conversation with Toni Morrison, *The New Republic,* March 21, 1981, 25-29.

Black Women Writers at Work, ed. Claudia Tate. New York: Continuum, 1984.

Race in Relation to Gender and Class: *The Bluest Eye*

K. SUMANA
Canberra

> Her blackness is the antithesis of a creamy white skin, her lips are thick, her hair is kinky, and short she is, in fact the antithesis of American beauty . . . in this country she is ugly . . . when to her physical unattractiveness added a discouraging, deprecating mother—family—environment into which she is born, there can be no doubt that she will develop a damaged self-concept and an impairment of her feminine narcissism.
>
> Calvin Hernton, *Sex and Racism in America*

> The attempt to become "white" intensifies rather than mitigates the Negro woman's frustration in white world. No amount of pain, powder, and hair straightner can erase all the things in the black woman's background that make her femininity and aesthetic appreciation of herself as a beauty capable of attracting men. The Negro woman becomes ashamed of what she is.
>
> William Grier and Price Cobbs, *Black Rage*

In his turn-of-the-century definition of double-consciousness, W.E.B. DuBois, in his book, *The Souls of Black Folk,* gauges the deleterious impact of racism on cultural self-consciousness and identity. The term, 'double-consciousness,' refers to two distinct realities—a psychological conflict between opposing cultural world views and debilitating resolution in which externally derived and distorted perceptions of the self constitute a single, but alienated self-consciousness. DuBois further notes: "It is a peculiar sensation, this double-consciousness, this sense of always looking at one's self through the eyes of others, of measuring one's soul by the tape of a world that looks on in amused contempt and pity."[1]

This observation illuminates the socio-political implications behind Toni Morrison's first novel, *The Bluest Eye* (1970). Inspired by the climate of revolution and evolving black consciousness of the Sixties, a period characterized by an almost evangelical struggle for personal and racial identity, Morrison chooses, as the basic theme and subject of her first major work, the obsession of blacks with an American standard of beauty that seems both inescapable and destructive. And, as Morrison herself states, "the concept of physical beauty as a virtue is one of the dumbest, most pernicious and destructive ideas of the western world."[2]

The Bluest Eye is a tragic tale about a young, black girl's desire for the bluest eyes, the symbol for her of what it means to be beautiful and, therefore, worthy in society. The pivotal idea in the novel is the domination of blacks by the existing American standards of beauty—blue eyes, blonde hair and white skin. It deals honestly and sensitively with the damaging influence of white standards and values on the lives of black people. It portrays in poignant terms the tragic condition of blacks in a racist America. It examines how the ideologies, perpetuated by the institutions controlled by the dominant group, influence the making of self-image of black women, thereby exposing the devastation caused by white cultural domination in the lives of African Americans. As Elizabeth Jane Way observes, Morrison's "stunning insight reveals the disrupted emotions produced by living in a world where white standards and goals are presented to blacks as uniquely important and, at the same time, impossible for them to achieve."[3] In short, the novel lays bare the victimization of black people within the context of racist social order.

Although *The Bluest Eye*, at the core, is about the contradictions fostered by racism, sexism, and class distinctions affecting the black girls in white America, Morrison, at this stage of her literary career, considers racism the African's primary obstacle. For, as Doreatha Drummond Mbalia points out, when this novel was written, "Morrison's level of consciousness about the primary cause of the nature of the African's oppression in the United States as well as in the rest of the world was considerably weak, for she not only subordinates the role of economics to racism, but also neglects to show a causal relationship between them, that an exploitive economic system gives rise to racist ideology."[4] Naturally, the whole emphasis of the novel is on racism which "abstracts the colour of the living body into non-colours of extreme value, black and white, within this organization; black represents the shade of evil, the devil's aspect, night, separation, loneliness, sin, dirt, excrement, the inside of the body, and white represents the mark of good, the token of innocence, purity, cleanliness, spirituality, virtue and hope."[5] *The Bluest Eye,* thus, makes one of the most powerful attacks on the relationship between western standards of female beauty and the psychological oppression of black women.

The thesis of the novel is that racism devastates the self-image of the African female in general and African female child in particular. At the crux of the novel is the society's need for a pariah, the need of its members to have someone to look down upon and, therefore, enhance one's constantly threatened sense of worth. The novel succinctly expresses the vulnerability of poor black girls and how easily they can become the pariahs in a white society.

Furthermore, the novel reveals a consistency in Morrison's vision of the human condition, particularly in her preoccupation with the effect of community on the individual's achievement and retension of an integrated, acceptable self. In treating this subject, she draws recurrently on myth and legend for story pattern and characters, returning repeatedly to the theory of 'quest' as a motivating and organising device. Moreover, the theme of quest is always underscored by ironic insights and intensely evocative imagery. An exploration of these distinguishing qualities—technical and thematic—enhances one's appreciation of Morrison's achievement in her maiden attempt.

The Bluest Eye is not only the story of the destructive effects of interracial prejudice upon impressionable black girls in the Midwest, but also a succinct account of African American folk culture in process. Through subtle ways, Morrison suggests that the vibrancy of the folk culture persists through the fortunes and misfortunes of the characters and that it serves to baptize them into kinship with each other. The novel is about cultural beliefs which are the essence of folkloristic transmission. The belief that black was not valuable or beautiful was, however, one of the cultural hindrances to black people throughout their history in America.

II

This belief informs the tragedy of Pecola Breedlove who is at the centre of *The Bluest Eye.* Pecola comes from a poor family that is virtually cut off from the normal life of a community. The Breedloves despise themselves because they believe in their own unworthiness which is translated into ugliness for the women of that family. Pecola's mother, Pauline, who works as a domestic servant in a beautiful house, hates the ugliness of her house, her daughter, her family and herself and, what is worse, blames her sense of unworthiness on being black and poor. Having inherited the myth of unworthiness, the Breedloves can only live the outlined saga to its expected conclusion. The novel, therefore, becomes a myth that defines human worth and explores the potential greatness of the people who are waylaid by the beliefs they have adopted from outsiders.

The mythology Morrison explores in *The Bluest Eye* centres upon the standard of beauty by which white women are judged in America. They are taught that their blond hair, blue eyes, and creamy skins are not only wonderful but are the surface manifestations of the very best character God and nature ever moulded. Oral traditions bolstered by literature and other media have solidified their pedestalization. We see in the novel how Pecola is forced to long for blue eyes like those of white children, so that she would also be loved and accepted by both whites and blacks:

> Pecola Breedlove is a young black girl driven literally insane by the pressure toward absolute physical beauty in a culture whose white standards of beauty—are impossible for her to meet, though no less alluring and demanding. Surrounded by cultural messages

> that she is ugly by definition, she can achieve peace only by retreating into schizophrenia.[6]

Pecola's yearning for blue eyes—the white American standard of beauty—is an external manifestation of the internal need to be loved and accepted by the white community. Pecola, who never considers herself beautiful, is all admiration for the eyes of the whites which she longs to possess through some miracle. Her obsession with physical beauty leads to disastrous consequences. Morrison says:

> When the strength of a race depends on its beauty, when the focus is turned to how one looks as opposed to what one is, we are in trouble. . . . The concept of physical beauty as a virtue is one of the dumbest, most pernicious and destructive ideas of the western world, and we should have nothing to do with it. Physical beauty has nothing to do with our past, present or future. Its absence or presence was only important to "them," the white people who used it for anything they wanted.[7]

But, Pecola never realises this, being as she has been under the spell of white cultural domination. All that she has experienced is repeated rejection and brutalization. Even more chillingly, her parents, who have never experienced nurturing love, do not know how to love, and so they cannot give their children a sense of worth. This predicament of her parents is also the outcome of racial injustice.

The racial predicament in which Pecola and her parents are placed is exquisitely expressed in the main body of the novel which is divided into four chapters named after four seasons—Autumn. Winter, Spring and Summer. And, we are prepared for this scheme by Claudia's introductory statement in which she relates the failure of the marigolds to sprout with the death of Pecola's baby. Nature images are constant throughout the book and help in organizing its structure. Interspersed with this are the physical and psychological events that lead to the rape of Pecola by her father and to her ill-fated pregnancy. The division into seasons, beginning with autumn, charts the development of events that form the plot of the novel.

The use of names of seasons, intended to indicate the major parts of *The Bluest Eye,* aids Morrison in telling her story. By beginning the novel with autumn, she suggests to us that the world of the novel is topsy-turvy. Spring usually symbolizes the beginning of things, the time of birth and rebirth. Winter, in contrast, is the time of death and decay. And, summer, commonly associated with life in full bloom and ripeness, is a time of death, life in its final moments. These seasonal divisions help the reader in understanding the fundamental decadence of life of the Africans living in the United States. They help in telling Morrison's story of the warped psyche of an adolescent African female living in a racist society.

Morrison begins the novel most innovatively with a passage in the simplest possible language, the language of a prep school reader:

> Here is the house. It is green and white. It has a red door. It is very pretty. Here is the family. Mother, Father, Dick and Jane live in the green-and-white house, they are very happy. See Jane. She has a red dress. She wants to play. Who will play with Jane? See the cat. It goes meow-meow. Come and play. Come play with Jane. The kitten will not play. See Mother. Mother is very nice. Mother, will you play with Jane? Mother laughs. Laugh, Mother, laugh. See Father. He is big and strong. Father, will you play with Jane? Father is smiling. Smile, Father, smile. See the dog. Bow-wow goes the dog, Do you want play with Jane? See the dog run. Run, dog, run. Look, look. Here comes a friend. The friend will play with Jane. They will play a good game. Play, Jane, play.[8]

The passage is subsequently but immediately repeated twice in two entirely different ways. The second version repeats the same passage exactly, but without capitals or punctuation:

> Here is the house it is green and white it has a red door it is very pretty here is the family mother father dick and jane live in the green and white house they are very happy see jane she has a red dress she wants to play who will play with jane see the cat it goes meow-meow come and play come play with jane the kitten will not play see mother mother is very nice mother will you play with jane mother laughs laugh mother laugh see father he is big and strong

> father will you play with jane father is smiling smile father smile see the dog bowwow goes the dog do you want play with jane see the dog run run dog run look look here comes a friend the friend will play with jane they will play a good game play Jane play. (1)

In the third version, the wording of the paragraph is likewise unaltered, but without boundaries of spacing or punctuation:

> Hereisthehouseitisgreenandwhiteithasareddooritisveryprettyhereist hefamilymotherfatherdickandjaneliveinthegreenandwhitehousethey areveryhappyseejaneshehasareddressshewantstoplaywhowillplaywi thjaneseethecatitgoesmeowmeowcomeandplaycomeplaywithjaneth ekittenwillnotplayseemothermotherisverynicemotherwillyouplaywi thjanemotherlaughslaughmotherlaughseefatherheisbigandstrongfat herwillyouplaywithjanefatherissmilingsmilefathersmileseethedogb owwowgoesthedogdoyouwantplaywithjaneseethedogrundogrunloo klookherecomesafriendthefriendwillplaywithjanetheywillplayagoo dgameplayjaneplay. (2)

The passage which is completely run together like one long collection of consonants and vowels seeming to signify nothing, invariably reminds us of a similar but far longer passage in Beckett's play, *Waiting for Godot,* through which Lucky thinks.

The three versions of the unique opening paragraph of *The Bluest Eye* may be said to be symbolic of the three life styles that Morrison explores in the novel either directly or by implication. The first version of the paragraph indicates an alien white world, represented by the Dick-Jane family that intrudes into the lives of the black children. The second version represents the life-style of the MacTeer family which survives the poverty and the racism that it encounters in Ohio. The third distorted run-on-version of the paragraph stands for the Breedlove family which lives in a deformed world being exploited by the ruling class. Thus, the simulated "here is the house" passage, with its variants, serves several purposes as Klotman points out: "First and foremost it serves as a synopsis of the tale that is to follow revealing the psychic confusion of the novel. It also serves as an ironic comment on a society which educated and unconsciously socializes its children like Pecola with callous regard for the cultural richness and diversity of its people."[9]

On top of that, in the third version of the paragraph, the individual space between two words disappears as it does in the novel. The father intrudes on and violates the child's space. The clear structure of the story book world is wrecked as Pecola's life is wrecked. The cat and dog motif, for instance, appears in a sinister form in the novel. The black cat has blue eyes like Pecola which haunt her. And, the dog writhes as it dies of poison, the sign that Pecola must look for in order that her eyes become blue. The "friend" who comes to "play with Jane" is the invented friend who comes to play with Pecola as she enters the world of insanity. Jacqueline de Weever hardly exaggerates when, in her brilliant article, "The Inverted World of Toni Morrison's *The Bluest Eye* and *Sula*," she quips: "all the elements of the novel are here."[10]

In *The Bluest Eye,* there are three "minor" African families who, for their social status and economic and political advancement, exploit their own brethren in order to become close to the ruling class. One such family is the Peals. Although the reader is introduced to only one member of this family, Maureen, her appearance, behavioural patterns and remarks offer sufficient glimpses of consciousness of the Peals. By dissociating itself from the African community, the second family, Geraldine Louis and Louis Junior also nurture the aspirations of the ruling class. They consider themselves to be 'coloured,' signifying some nebulous group of Africans who are neither European nor African: "Coloured people were neat and quiet; niggers were dirty and loud." (67) The third family, the Whitcombs, are so obsessed with the physical appearances of Europeans that they jeopardize their mental stability by intermarrying, only to maintain some semblance of whiteness. Here Morrison seems to be more interested in developing the skin-colour conflict or race conflict than the gender and class conflicts.

III

Even though Morrison is conscious of the role class-aspirations play in the minor families, she often discusses these aspirations as if they were interracial prejudices based on skin colour rather than class conflicts. Her discussions on class conflicts, which are couched within are overshadowed by her discussions on racial prejudices. As a result, the focus in *The Bluest Eye* is on racism as a primary problem confronting African people.

There are many incidents in the novel which hurt Pecola into a feeling of isolation and pain because of her race. To mention but a few, her encounter with a fifty-two-year-old white storekeeper makes her aware that for many people, she does not really exist. Let alone the whites, even the black boys taunt her, at school. She becomes the scapegoat for their own humiliation and pain. Junior, a black boy, makes her the scapegoat for his own pain. Pecola's mother, who works as a housekeeper in a white family, lavishes all her love and affection on her employer's children, reserving her jibes and slaps for her own hapless daughter. The reason for the tendency of black people to harass other black people is, perhaps, self-hatred induced by white hegemony. White standards corrupted the minds of black people in such a way that black people have developed self-hatred:

> It was as though some mysterious all-knowing master has given each one a cloak of ugliness to wear, and they had each accepted it without question. The master had said, "you are ugly people." They looked about themselves and saw nothing to contradict the statement, saw, in fact, support for it leaning at them from every billboard, every move, every glance. (28)

The ultimate act of brutalization and betrayal for Pecola comes when Cholly, her own father, rapes her. Cholly's unnatural rape of Pecola could be interpreted "as a pathetic attempt to return to the heady days of first love when his very presence essentially created another human being." Cholly turns to Pecola in hopes of rescuing her from the dehumanizing glare of all white people and a subsequently loveless existence. His tenderness and protectiveness, however, unfortunately slip into lust and rage which he directs at Pecola and all those like her "who bore witness to his failure, his importance. The one whom he had not been able to protect to spare to cover from the round moon glow of the flashlight." (119) Cholly's rape of Pecola is, thus, the distortion of his love for Pecola. Pecola's stillborn child is not only a symbol of his personal violation but of the fettered life she has been made to live.

In sum, Pecola is the central scapegoat of the novel, *The Bluest Eye.* For, she is not only made a scapegoat by her parents but also by the mulattos in the novel, and even by the narrator, Claudia, a once-caring friend, shuns Pecola in the end. At the end of her assessment, Claudia recognizes Pecola's role as scapegoat:

> All of us—all who knew her—felt so wholesome after we cleaned ourselves on her. We were so beautiful when we stood astride her ugliness. Her simplicity decorated us, her guilt sanctified us, her pain made us glow with health, her awkwardness made us think we had a sense of humour. Her inarticulateness made us generous. Even her waking dreams we used—to silence our own nightmares. And she let us, and thereby deserved our contempt. We honed our egos on her, padded our characters with her frailty, and yawned in the fantasy of our strength. (163)

Clearly, Claudia maintains that Pecola is equally responsible for the role in which she is cast. In the end, she holds Pecola partially responsible for her unfulfilled life.

Thus, as a black girl, Pecola undergoes all the traumatic experiences. She wants to rise up out of the pit of her blackness and see the world with blue eyes, but the pity is that she is not allowed to. Excluded from reality by racial discrimination and inequality, Pecola goes mad, fantasizing that her eyes have turned blue and so fitted her for the world. She has lost her balance of mind. As Cynthia Davies points out, "Pecola is the epitome of the victim in a world that reduces persons to objects and then makes them feel inferior as objects."[12]

Morrison's purpose in showing us the psychic state and the resultant behaviour of Pecola under the pressure of white domination is to expose the vicious genocidal effects of racism on the black girls, thereby raising the question of what it means to be black in a racist society. As Shelby Steel puts it, "to be black was to be a victim; therefore not to be a victim was not to be a black."[13]

The experiences of black children growing up amid the standards of the larger, white society are conveyed through a number of images which are both grotesque and ordinary. Blue eyes, which are Pecola's unfulfilled dream, seem to stem from the background in surrealistic dominance: "Pecola Breedlove believes that exchanging her brown eyes for blue ones will make her beautiful and loved. The people who influence Pecola as she grows up are clearly the source for this harmful idea. As appearance approved by dominant white society, such people damage both themselves and others."[14] The tangible Shirley Temple doll, with which the girls play, has blue eyes. Furthermore, the little daughter of the employer of Pecola's mother has blue eyes. The image remains, in the same way like a painfully blinding light, an instrument of torture throughout the novel.

The Shirley Temple Cup and the Mary Jane candies allow Pecola to carry the image through her very being, to become one with it for short periods of time. However, she believes that after obtaining the bluest eyes, the most irreproachable feature in the world, will allow permanent union with those currently transitory features. Hating her black self, she yearns for blue eyes because she believes that will extinguish her position as pariah and give her love and security that are desperately missing from her life. Thus, Pecola sincerely believes that blue eyes are a panacea for all her ills:

> It had occurred to Pecola some time ago that if her eyes . . . were different . . . she herself would be different. . . . If she looked different, beautiful, maybe (her father) would be different, and (her mother) too. Maybe they'd say, why look at pretty-eyed Pecola. We mustn't do bad things in front of those pretty eyes. (34)

The blue eyes thus become the metonymical representation of the myth. Having blue eyes means having everything—love, acceptance, friends, family—in short, a truly enviable place in the society.

The white baby dolls, so antithetical to negroid features are presented to little black girls like Claudia and, what is more, they are judged to be their most sought-after wish. Claudia muses: "Adults, older girls, shops, magazines, newspapers, window signs—all the world had agreed that a blue-eyed, yellow-haired, pink-skinned doll was what every girl treasured." (14) To the parents, dolls are unfulfilled longings of their own childhoods, and Mrs. MacTeer and other adults cannot understand Claudia's destroying of them. She tears them apart in an attempt to find the source of their loveliness and what makes the world treasure them.

To illustrate the depth of Pecola's motivation for the quest for blue eyes, Morrison uses several characters and incidents to depict the kind of world into which Pecola has been born and the effect of the myth upon her. We see how Pecola's own mother, Pauline, who is, in effect, a black mammy to the wealthy blonde girl doll who lives in a beautiful house, consciously and unconsciously passes on certain attitudes toward colour to her daughter. For instance, when Pecola comes, along with other black girls, to the kitchen of the white home where Pauline works, to pick up wash, she drops a hot pan of blueberry pie and dirties the floor. Instead of comforting her daughter, who has been burnt, Pauline spits out words like "rotten pieces of apple" at the black girls and turns to hushing and soothing the tears of the little pink-and-yellow girl who is upset by the accident. Pecola is made to feel ugly and stupid beside the little white girl, who represents everything that is 'right.'

Pauline's dominant characteristic, however, is her overwhelming self-hatred, which precludes struggle of any kind. She is aware of the turning wheels of racial oppression in her life, but she makes no effort to stop the turning. Instead, she oils the axles and polishes the spokes so that the wheels turn more smoothly, more rapidly, and without interruption. She wears her maid's uniform with pride and bows low to the racist demands of the white Fisher family. She does not bemoan her lot in the house of whiteness and plenty. Rather, she smiles as she plays the role of surrogate mother for Fishers' young daughter, Polly. She struts as she surveys the results of her handiwork—an immaculate house filled with enticing aromas of homemade pies and other dishes the Fishers enjoy. In her storefront house, irritating and melancholy in appearance, she is irredeemably ugly. In the Fisher home, she is beautiful and important, made so by the magic of service to white people.

We find resemblance between Pauline and the traditional image of the black mammy. The black mammy is a pervasive character in white American fiction. She appears as Disley in *The Sound and the Fury,* Calpurnia in Carson McCuller's *A Member of the Wedding*, Berenice in Harper Lee's *To Kill a Mockingbird,* and simply 'Mammy' in Margaret Mitchell's *Gone with the Wind.* Whatever her name, and whatever the artistic merit of the book that contains her, she is always "a dutiful black female servant, who attempts to keep white families from cutting their souls on the shattered pieces of their morally bankrupt lives, while able to place only a thin and soiled bandage on the open wounds of her own black family."[15]

IV

The poignancy of Pecola's victimization emanates not only from the racism and resulting inter-racial conflicts, but also from the intraracial conflicts related to colour, firmly rooted in white racist myths. As damaging as the white criterion of beauty that denies Pecola a positive sense of self are the values of light-skinned Maureen Peal, whose sense of superiority is associated with her colour. Morrison's narrator is clear about how the Breedlove's appearance becomes problematic. It is not their ugliness, but their conviction of their ugliness that makes the difference.

Pecola experiences the greatest damage from intraracial prejudice, however, at the hands of her abusive, negligent parents. We are told that even her mother, Pauline, has decided at the time of Pecola's birth that she is an ugly child. To be sure, the onus of Pecola's negativity rests initially with her family's failure to provide socialization, identity, love and security that are essential for healthy growth and development. The emptiness of her parents's lives and their own negative self-images are particularly hurtful. Not only does their socio-economic status as poor blacks set them on the periphery of society, but their perception of themselves as ugly isolates them further, resulting in their self-hatred which is the most destructive element in their lives. Morrison's discourse, thus, strongly suggests that Pecola's alienation and sense of unworthiness emerge not solely from the 'others' definition but also from her own inability 'to transcend the resulting reification.'

Morrison's condemnation of racism in *The Bluest Eye* is, thus, tempered by the recognition of the unnatural position of blacks in a racist society. At the end of the novel, Morrison does not suggest that the victim is to blame for all that happens, in every instance. She is, however, exploring a larger question of 'being' through the characters of this novel. In spite of the existence of 'the other,' what is important is each individual's willingness to take responsibility for his or her own life. Morrison does not suggest that external forces, such as racism and sexism, are unimportant. Neither the indictment of white society for its oppression of blacks nor the indictment of blacks for their treatment of women is her sole interest or focus. As W. Lawrence rightly notes: "Morrison is concerned with the ontological structures and mythological thought systems that blacks develop to define and reinforce their definition of self and existence."[16]

V

One should not, however, fail to note that Pecola suffers not only because of her race but also because of her gender. In other words, she suffers both as a black and a female. Just as blacks as a group are relegated to an underclass in America by virtue of their race, so are women relegated to a separate caste by virtue of their sex. "Just as white people have created and maintained a racist culture, so have men created and maintained a sexist culture."[17] The women find themselves in a double jeopardy of race and gender. As a racial being, she is asked to relinquish her individual and cultural ways and follow white dictates and as a gender being she is socialized to subordinate her femininity and remain subsumed in the orbit of patriarchy. Morrison seems to move her examination of Pecola's life back and forth from the axis of race to that of gender.

Since black women find themselves in a double jeopardy of race and gender, any study on them must be related not only to their racial or colonial experience, but also to the experience arising out of their femininity. Having got to share oppression equally with both the groups, blacks and women, the black woman remains a victim of both racism and sexism. That is why Pecola in the novel experiences dependency, repression, internalization, alienation and all such neuroses not only as a racial being but as a woman as well. As a woman, she shares almost the same experiences and undergoes the same subjugation and marginalization which any other woman would experience under patriarchal imperialism.

Woman in a patriarchal society is the socially sanctioned 'other' and her psyche is the product of social constructs. As Simon de Beauvoir points out: "One is not born, but rather becomes woman. . . . It is civilization as a whole that produces this creature, intermediate between male and eunuch, which is described as feminine."[18] From the moment of birth, when the conventional first question is asked regarding the gender of the child, a female is constantly bombarded with social images, rewards, and punishments that are designed to ensure that she does not develop any quality associated with the other half of humanity. She must be "feminine" and restrict herself to a 'woman's place.' It is the patriarchal civilization that defines woman as a marginalized creature. Her definition and differentiation is always made in deference to man. A woman is never considered an autonomous self, but as just incidental, the inessential and an appendage to man.

In *The Bluest Eye,* black girlhood assumes tragic propensities when it borrows identity models from the mandates of white culture and from the malevolent parental mirrors as well. Like many other contemporary black women writers such as Maya Angelou, Gwendolyn Brooks and Paule Marshall, Morrison believes in the anxiety black girls and women feel about and what their mirrors tell them. For instance, Maud Martha, in Brooks' *Maud Martha,* is a woman who is aware of her own reality, and this is evident from what she understands of her husband's mind:

> it's my color that makes him mad. I try to shut my eyes to that, but it's no good. What I am inside, what is really me, he likes okay. But he keeps looking at my color—which is like a wall. He has to jump over it in order to meet and touch what I've got for him. He has to jump away up high in order to see it. He gets awful tired of that jumping.[19]

Brooks has shown us a courageous, simple black woman who is able to make the best of her life, despite her race and sex.

Morrison too holds that girls growing up black and female in a white society often experience the malady of internalizing the belief that an aesthetically pleasing image is what constitutes the necessary precondition for receiving love and security. Clearly, sexism and racism are systems of societal and psychological restrictions that have critically affected the lives of African-American women. Since sex and race have been so interrelated in the history of America, it is not surprising that when black women published novels, they necessarily reflected that relationship.

From a feminist perspective, *The Bluest Eye* is a study of the various degrees of fulfillment women experience as women. Pauline is at one end of the spectrum. Other women characters are less obviously deprived, at least economically. Some are "comfortable" completely immersed in the motherhood and find peace in resignation to the limitations of their lives. Mrs. MacTeer, whose daughters befriend Pecola, is such a woman. She rears her family in rooms "peopled by roaches and mice" and open around windows and doors to the cold wind. She makes ends meet by taking in borders and by "watching every possibility of excess." Like other women in the community, she dreads the "real terror of life," being put "outdoors," and "having no place to go." Claudia MacTeer explains the reality of her mother and other women in the community: "Being a minority in both caste and class we moved about . . . on the hem of life, struggling to consolidate our weakness and hang on, or to creep singly up into the major folds of the garment." (18)

The second group of women, whom Morrison calls the "sugar-brown mobile girls," lives in better neighbourhoods where everyone is employed and where there are fine houses with porch swings and sunflowers and pots of bleeding hearts. These women are poor imitations of what they believe whiteness to be. They have smooth hands and slim ankles. They wash with "orange-colored lifebuoy soap, dust themselves with Cashmere Bouquet and soften their skin with Jergen's Lotion." (68) Though they marry and have children, they find sex repulsive. At land-grant colleges and normal schools where they are educated, they learn "how to do the white man's work with refinement . . . how to instruct black children in obedience and how to develop thrift, patience, high morals, and good manners." (64) They are fake and frigid women who deny their blackness and their sexuality, who tried to get rid of the funkiness:

> The dreadful funkiness of passion, the funkiness of nature, the funkiness of the wide range of human emotions. Wherever it erupts, this funk they wipe it away; where it crusts, they dissolve it; wherever it drips, flowers or clings, they find it and fight it until it dies. They fight this battle all the way to the grave. (64)

The third category of women Morrison depicts in the novel have no desire for prosperity or rootedness of any kind. These women are prostitutes, embittered and frigid in lovemaking because they choose to be. And they choose to be prostitutes because they hated men, all men, without shame, apology or discrimination. They abused their visitors with a scorn grown mechanical from use. Black men, white men, Puerto Racians, Mexicans, Jews, Poles, whatever—all were inadequate and weak, all came under their jaundiced eyes and were the recipients of their disinterested wrath. (43) Regardless of the category in which her women characters exist, they are removed from the possibility of self-knowledge, self-expression, and freedom.

VI

But, as Donald B. Gibson observes, "the novel has its class ramifications too."[20] Pecola suffers not only because she is a black and a female but also because she is poor. Pecola is poor and so too, may be slightly better off is the MacTeer family which takes her in. The contrast between even the MacTeer house and the white house where Pauline works, is not just a contrast between blacks and whites but between poverty and affluence. Critics like Gloria Wade-Gayles see class "not as urgent as race and sex in black women's reality for class oppression cuts across racial and sexual lines, and is, therefore, not unique to black women."[21] Even if we do not see ethnicity as a mask behind which people conceal their class position both from each other and from themselves, even if we realize the importance of racial and ethnic values, we cannot ignore the class issue. No doubt, the African-American women writers—Frances Harper, Jessie Fauset, Nella Larsen, Zora Neale Hurston, Paule Marshall, Alice Walker, and Gloria Naylor—have dealt with it, but they and many of their critics lay more stress on race and gender than on class.

Although Morrison's class analysis is immature at this point, she is at least conscious of a limited role that economics plays in the exploitation of African people. It is Morrison's growing awareness of the inherent characteristics of capitalism that help her understand that racism is an integral part of the capitalist mode of production. There is ample evidence to prove that racism is a by-product of capitalism. However, to state that racism is the consequence of the European's quest for greater profits, is not to imply that racism has not ultimately become a concomitant reason for oppressing African people. In the words of Rodney, "oppression of African people on purely racial grounds accompanied, strengthened and became indistinguishable from oppression for economic reasons."[22]

Though Morrison has rightly understood the concept of beauty from an intellectual point of view, she could not understand that even this concept would change depending on the racial make up of the dominant class. Her misconception of class-consciousness at this point in her writing career might be due to her lack of understanding of three important factors. First, the ruling class, whether of European, African or Asian descent, possesses the major instruments of economic production and distribution as well as the means of establishing its socio-cultural dominance. Second, possessing such means, the ruling class uses and promotes its own image as a measurement of beauty for the entire society. Third, the success of this promotion ensures the continual dominance of the ruling class. This is amply endorsed when Nkrumah says: "Race is inextricably linked with class exploitation; in a racist-capitalist power structure, capitalist exploitation and race oppression are complementary, the removal of one ensures the removal of the other."[23]

VII

Thus, Pecola Breedlove in the novel is oppressed not only racially, but also sexually and on the basis of class distinction. Associated with her condition are funk, violence, ugliness and poverty, symbolized by her storefront house. The mother's own internalization of the desirable woman as beautiful, well-taken-care-of and cuddled, results in Pauline's rejection of her own daughter, Pecola, who cannot possibly obtain such a standard not only because of her blackness but also because of her poverty. Nevertheless, Morrison's focus is on racism in as much as she considers, at the initial stage of her career, racism the primary obstacle of the Africans in America.

To conclude, a close study of *The Bluest Eye* from the viewpoint of the interaction of race, gender, and class reveals Morrison's low level of gender and class-consciousness at the beginning of her literary career. Initially she thinks that racism is the only form of oppression of Africans in the white-dominated society. Though classism and sexism, the other primary causes of oppression, are also treated in the novel, they are overshadowed by Morrison's emphasis on racism.

NOTES

1. W.E.B. DuBois, *The Souls of Black Folk* (New York: Avon Books, 1965), 14.
2. Toni Morrison, "Behind the Making of *The Black Book,*" *Black World,* 23 (1974), 89.

3. Elizabeth Janeway, *Women's Literature,* in Hoffman (1979), 383.
4. Doreatha Drummond Mabalia, *Toni Morrison's Developing Class-Consciousness* (Selinsgrove: Susquehanna Univ. Press, 1991), 28.
5. Joel Kovel, *White Racism: A Psychohistory* (New York: Columbia University Press, 1984), 232.
6. Raymond Hedin, "The Structuring of Emotion in Black American Fiction," *Novel: A Forum on Fiction,* 16, 1 (1982), 49-50.
7. Toni Morrison, "Behind the Making of *The Black Book*," 89.
8. Toni Morrison, *The Bluest Eye* (London: Pan, 1970), 1.
9. Klotman Phyllis, "Dick and Jane and Shirley Temple Sensibility in *The Bluest Eye*," *Black American Literature Forum*, 13 (1979), 124.
10. Jacqueline de Weerer, "The Inverted World of Toni Morrison's *The Bluest Eye* and *Sula,*" *CLA Journal,* 22 (1979), 21.
11. Denise Heinze, *The Dilemma of "Double-Consciousness": Toni Morrison's Novels* (Athens and London: The University of Georgia Press, 1993), 74.
12. Cynthia Davis, "Self, Society and Myth in Toni Morrison's Fiction," *Contemporary Literature,* 23, 3 (1982), 330.
13. Steel Shelby, "Black Consciousness in Perspective," *The American Review,* 33, 1 (1989), 58.
14. Elizabeth B. House, "Artists and the Art of Living: Order and Disorder in Toni Morrison's Fiction," *Modern Fiction Studies,* 34, 1 (1988), 29.
15. Denise Heinze, *The Dilemma of "Double-Consciousness,"* 72.
16. H. Lawrence, *Discourse and the Other* (Durham: Duke University Press, 1986), 133.
17. Calvin C. Hernton, *The Sexual Mountain and Black Women Writers* (New York: Anchor, 1987), 10.
18. Simon de Beauvoir, *The Second Sex* (London: Picador, 1988), 16
19. Brooks Gwendolyn, *Maud Martha* (N.Y.: Harper, 1953), 87-88.
20. Gibson B. Donald, "The Text and Countertext in Toni Morrison's *The Bluest Eye*," *Literature and Interpretation Theory,* 1-2 (USA: Gordon and Breach Science Publishers), 171.
21. Gloria Wade-Gayles, *No Crystal Stair: Visions of Race and Sex in Black Women's Fiction* (New York: The Pilgrim Press, 1984), 7.
22. Walter Rodney, *How Europe Underdeveloped Africa* (Dar es Salaam: Tanzania Publishing House, 1972), 100.
23. Kwame Nkrumah, *Class Struggle in Africa* (New York: International Publishers, 1970), 27.

Theme of Silence in *The Bluest Eye*

M. KANNAN
Saraswathi Narayanan College, Madurai

The history of the American black is the history of a long strife to attain self-conscious manhood, to merge his double self into a better and truer self. In this merging, he wishes neither of the older selves to be lost. He would not Africanize America, for America has too much to teach the world and Africa. He would not bleach his black soul in a flood of white Americanism, for he knows that "Negro Blood" has a message for the world. He simply wishes to make it possible for a man to be both a Negro and an American without being cursed and spit upon by his fellows, without having the doors of opportunity closed roughly in his face. The Negro mind reaches out as yet to nothing but American wants, American ideas. But this forced attempt to build his Americanism on race values is a unique social experiment, and its ultimate success is impossible except through the fullest sharing of American culture and institutions. The racialism of the Negro is no limitation or reservation with respect to American life. It is only a constructive effort to build the obstructions in the stream of his progress into an efficient social energy and power.

The black American novel begins with Clotelle or the Coloured Heroine (1853) by William Wells Brown. Clotelle has always been regarded as a pivotal book in black letters in so far as many critics have used it as a departure point for two directions in nineteenth century black writing—the tradition of black social criticism and the novel. These forms must be understood in terms of the catastrophe of American slavery, detailed fully by Frederick Douglass and others in slave narratives that are the ancestral roots of black fiction. Black literature is basically a bloody history of atrocity, of stripping a people of cultural identity, then grotesquely caricaturing them in the national white imagination. Historically, the black literature is a literature of protest but in silence. Between 1885 and 1900, 2500 blacks were lynched; an average of about one murder every third day. This was the time of Douglass's death and of Washington's ascension and of repression, White Southern reaction in the form of Jim Crow legislation, "black codes" and revivified racial stereotypes. On the whole and in general, a nightmare. The black American writer begins his or her career with a "crisis of identity." If anything, black fiction is about the troubled quest for identity and liberty, the agony of social alienation, the longing for a real and at times a mythical home. Something similar to that of American writers in respect to their struggle to break with European culture and to carve out an "American" sense of selfhood.

Toni Morrison's works are fantastic earthly realism. Deeply rooted in history and mythology, her work resonates with mixtures of pleasure and pain, wonder and horror. Primal in their essence, her characters come at you with the force and beauty of gushing water, seemingly fantastic but as basic as the earth they stand on. They erupt, out of the world, sometimes gently, often with an intrigue that only a piercing intellect could create. Barbara Christian has made a thoughtful observation in this connection:

> Her novels, are rich then, not only in human characterizations but also in the signs, symbols, omens, sent by nature, wind and fire, robins as a plague in the spring, marigolds that won't sprout are as much characterizations in her novels as the human beings.[1]

Toni Morrison's *The Bluest Eye* presents a simple theme. The story of a black girl who wants blue eyes, a symbol of beauty and therefore of goodness and happiness:

> Pretty eyes, pretty eyes, pretty blue eyes, big blue pretty eyes. Run, Jip, run, Jip runs. Alice runs. They run with their blue eyes. Four blue eyes. Four pretty blue eyes blue-joy eyes, blue-like Mrs. For-

> est's blue blouse eyes. Morning glory-blue eyes. Alice-and-Jerry-blue-story book eyes.
>
> Each night, without fail, she prayed for blue eyes.[2]

This statement of the theme, though undercuts the tragic complexity of such a desire, and complexity is precisely what Morrison is able to impress us with in her first novel. It is true that blue eyes, blond hair, fair skin, are the symbols of beauty. Valued in the West, these are proclaimed by romantic novels, movies billboards and the reactions of people to golden objects. But can one really understand the core of that myth and the value connotations it embodies? This simple theme, the desire of a black girl for blue eyes is a real and symbolic statement about the conflict between the good and the beautiful of two cultures and how it affects the psyche of the people within those cultures. The theme is at the base of the conflict of artistic and societal values between the Anglo-American and African American cultures, complicated by the psycho-political dominance of one culture over another. As such, this novel is a book about mythic, political and cultural mutilation as much as it is a book about race and sex hatred which the victims accept silently.

The Bluest Eye begins with prose familiar to a few generations of Americans, black and white:

> Here is the house. It is green and white. It has a red door. It is very pretty. Here is the family. Mother, Father, Dick and Jane live in the green and white house. They are very happy. (2)

The speed with which Morrison uses words set the tonal modalities for the structure of this story about Pecola Breedlove and her mother and father; about Claudia and Friend MacTeer and their mother and father; about Junior and his mother, Geraldine, and his father, about Maureen Peal, and her mother and father, about Henry, whores and of course the white family for whom Mrs. Breedlove works.

Claudia tells us in her introduction that this story takes place in the year 1940-41, from fall to fall, in the year when the baby of Pecola by her own father is born dead, in the year when the marigolds did not sprout. This nature image is the major structural element of the novel, for the book is divided into the seasons of the year, reflecting, sometimes ironically, on the tragedy of Pecola Breedlove. The use of Claudia as the child narrator of Pecola's sufferings seems to be one of Morrison's most brilliant strokes. As Pecola silently accepts all the pains and sufferings inflicted on her, Claudia becomes a way of giving voice to the graveness of Pecola's situation even as she herself is confronted with the same problems.

The main body of *The Bluest Eye* is divided into four chapters named after the seasons. Claudia relates the failure of the marigolds to sprout with the death of Pecola's baby. Nature images are constant throughout the book and help to organize its structure. At the centre of this nature construct are the physical and psychological events that lead to the rape of Pecola and to her ill-fated pregnancy, the divisions into seasons beginning with autumn chart that development of events. These events form the plot of this novel. Barbara Christian makes a pointed observation in this context:

> The seasons are not only surface movement in the novel; they are ironic and brutal comments on Pecola's descent into madness. In spring, for example, lovers flow into each other and fertility rites are cyclically re-enacted, as nature comes back to life; yet it is in that season that Pecola is raped by her father, the only love she is to know. The images of the seasons erupt every way in this book as nature itself remains constant, seemingly aloof, embodying the essence of memory. (141)

The Bluest Eye's first person narrator, Claudia, performs a similar act in rejecting white criteria of judgement when she is able to view her childhood which she had formerly conceived in a vocabulary of pain and degradation. Claudia's search for the source of white beauty is not confined solely to dolls. She says that the impulse to dismember white dolls gives way to "The truly horrifying thing."

> The transference of the same impulse to little white girls. The indifference with which I could have axed them was shaken only by my desire to do so. To discover what eluded me; the secret of the magic they weaved on others. What made people look at them and

> say, "AWWWWW" but not for me?, If I pinched them, their eyes—unlike the crazed glint of the baby doll's eyes—would fold in pain, and their cry would not be the sound of an icebox door, but a fascinating cry of pain.

Claudia's acts are motivated in the main by a need to locate the source of white beauty that is not immediately apparent to her. Claudia terminates her search for the source of white myths of superiority and replaces the violent urges she had previously directed at whites with "fraudulent love." But the suppression of violent urges by African Americans has significantly different implications for Morrison. For Morrison, the African American's humanity is not what is at stake, and "fraudulent love" of whites, the ultimate result of this rejection of violence is not human.

Pecola, soon after entering young womanhood, is raped by her father, goes mad and enters into the fantasy world of her newly acquired blue eyes. Pauline, her mother, finds haven, hope, life and meaning as servant to the white, bland, blue-eyed, clean, rich, family to which she dedicated her love and her respect for an orderly life that poverty does not afford from her kitchen throes, she comes to view the reality of her own family with disgust and almost hatred. Cholly knew his father for one day. He learned about caring through his grandmother who died when he was a boy. Loving, mischievous, romantic, searching and with the resiliency common to youth, one watches him decay into middle age. He tires in one drunken moment to recapture the poetry-dimly remembered when his soul was first moved. He had poetry first from Pauline and tried to capture it again from time to time. This time he tries with Pecola, his own daughter. It is around and through Pecola, the scanned and rejected girl who longs to be loved, that most of the main characters plod through a disparate pitiful search for meaning and personal definition.

Pecola is the passive centre of the novel, the one to whom things happen and whose only action is her prayers and receipt of blue eyes, renders her tragic. Her tragic flaw is her vulnerability and her generic ill luck to be born black and female to be born into the chasm between two cultures. She falls into that chasm's bottomlessness while others hag on by their toenails or seem to straddle it with one foot on either side, some times with an amazing lack of balance. The section in the book that belongs to her, the section in which the part of her with blue eyes covers with the part of her without them is not only a terror filled dialogue but is conclusive in its judgement of where all of the other characters really reside. Harrowed by an unfulfilled need for love, she finds a friend in the other part of herself, the part that can admire her newly acquired eyes. Morrison heads this sections "Look—Look HERECOMESAFRIEND THEFRIENDWILLPLAYWITHJANE. THEYWILLPLAYAGOOD GAME PLAYJANEPLAY." The friend will play with her only if she has the bluest eyes of all. Who is the fairest of us all?

In a sense, everyone in the town understands what has happened to Pecola, that the natural order has been inverted by the unnaturalness of human actions. They cannot look at her, because, as Claudia says, "All of as—all who knew her—felt so wholesome after we cleaned ourselves on her." They had all raped her. Claudia knows this that Pecola's madness was not only caused by the fatal love of her father, but was the "fault of the earth, the land of their town." One comes to know this not only through the terrifyingly connected structure of this novel but also through Morrison's style which moves both toward and beyond her characters at the same time.

The Bluest Eye is not only the story of the destructive effects of inter and intraracial prejudice upon impressionable black girls in the Midwest; it is also the study of African American folk culture in process. Through subtle ways, Morrison suggests that the vibrancy of the folk culture persists through the fortunes and misfortunes of the characters and it serves to baptize them into kinship with each other. From folk wisdom to the blues, from folk speech to myths and other beliefs, Lorain, Ohio, shares with historical black folk communities patterns of survival and coping traditions that comfort in times of loss, and beliefs that point to an enduring activity. One of the greatest beliefs in black communities during and after slavery is that the North is a freer place for black people economically and socially. For Pauline and

Cholly Breedlove, the myth of the North is temporarily a reality. They have a house and the money they need in Ohio. But Pauline's restlessness and Cholly's drinking eventually lead them to the triangular store front house that comes to epitomize their economic and mental state. When Pauline loses a tooth and gives up trying to imitate white movie heroines, she resigns herself to poverty and ugliness. When her children are born, she conditions them to see the North as the nightmare into which her dream has turned. In short, her trading of myth for reality becomes detrimental to her whole family. Their adherence to many folk beliefs is perceived as their inability to come out to face any kind of problem but to look inward and accept all ordeals and pains silently.

The novel opens with Claudia's remembrances of her mother's treatment for colds when she was growing up; a massage with Vicks salve, a bit to swallow, neck and chest wrapped in "hot flannel." All these were designed to induce sweating which was believed to be effective in reducing fevers. In black communities, where doctors were expensive or scarce, house remedies and items that could be purchased without prescription were relied on. Cholly's Aunt Jimmy wears her asafetida bag "around her neck," other older women in the community wrapped their heads in rags and their breasts in flannel." For them, belief in natural cures is a way of life, and they are not willing to part with their practices.

Pecola's basic wish for blue eyes ties her to all believers in fairlytales and other magical realms. It is Cinderella wanting to be transformed from char girl to belle of the ball, or Sleeping Beauty waiting a hundred years for the prince to awaken her. It is the classic tale of the ugly duckling turned beautiful swan, of the beast transformed through love and caring into the beautiful prince, of Sir Gawain's pig lady turned into a dazzling woman. While Pecola seems doomed whatever she does, she resorts to fantasy and is considered crazy. If she tries to live in the real world, there is no place for her and her desire for blue eyes ties her to many heroines of fairytales, and to many young girls who have wished for features other than the ones they have. While many of the later desires are no more than passing fancies, Pecola is more intense because she is never given the opportunity, in any realm such as house, school and playground to see anything positive in herself as she is. The patterns of caring and incorporation hinted at in some of the occurrences in the novel never reach her strongly enough to reshape her opinion of herself.

Lynching and castration are presented in *The Bluest Eye* as symbolic acts to go silent against sexual atrocities. Trueblood's presence inside his sexually inexperienced daughter's vagina is described in ways that suggest a significant symbolic import. The sharecropper's dream of sexual contact with a white woman while in the home of an affluent white man necessarily brings to mind images of lynching and castration of black men because of the threat of black male sexuality. Consequently, True blood's actual presence inside his daughter assumes less of an importance in the text than his dream encounter with an unnamed white woman. Morrison provides her description of incest with no such historically symbolic significance.

> (Cholly's) mouth troubled at the firm sweetness of the flesh. He closed his eyes, letting his fingers dig into her waist. The rigidness of her shocked body, the silence of her stunned throat, was better than Pauline's easy laughter had been. The confused mixture of his memories of Pauline and the doing of a wild and forbidden thing excited him, and bolt of desire rain down his genitals, giving it length, and softening the lips of his anus. Surrounding all of this lust was a border of politeness. He wanted to fuck her—tenderly. But the tenderness would not hold. The tightness of her vagina was more than he could bear. His soul seemed to slip down to his guts and fly out into her, and the gigantic thrust he made into her then provoked the only sound she made—a hollow such of air in the back of her throat. (128)

Though Morrison does give the incestuous male figure the capacity for sympathy, for example, the "border of politeness" that accompanies his lust—Cholly's "wild" "confused" act lacks the inscribed symbolic weight of Trueblood's transgression. The tight sexual space represents for Cholly the forbidden area that must be forcibly entered and excited. The text of *The Bluest Eye* informs us:

> Removing himself from her was so painful to him he cut it short and snatched his genitals out of the dry harbor of her vagina. (128)

In *The Bluest Eye*, Morrison had shown what can happen to a person alienated from positive black traditions. Pauline has lost her inner self, and the beauty of her own people. She tries to fill an aching void with the "White pictures shows" and makes efforts to look like Jean Harlow. Her daughter Pecola is further removed from community strengths and longs for "the bluest eyes" to gain entrance into a world that does not accept her.

Pauline and Pecola are the victims of both the sexist and racist oppression of an Anglo-Saxon standard of female beauty. The enemy of their oppression is not just men—black or white—but the entire majority culture that has perpetuated the standard in every channel available to them. Blonde hair and blue eyes according to this standard, are considered the prerequisites for female beauty and virtue.

A physical standard of beauty, Morrison believes, commercializes the virtue of all women, but as the inherent origin of the physical traits glamourized in this standard are Anglo-Saxon, it suggests that women who are not Anglo-Saxon are not beautiful and hence inferior.

Morrison shows Pauline and Pecola as victims of the sexist and racist oppression of an Anglo-Saxon standard of female beauty. Neither woman voices a self-conscious protest against this condition because the focus of Morrison's criticism in her first novel is not the way in which black women should rebel against prevailing social standards of beauty but on the society which makes such women victims of silence.

NOTES

1. Barbara Christian, *Black Women Novelists*, p. 137.
2. Toni Morrison, *The Bluest Eye* (New York: Holt, Rinehart and Winston, 1970), p. 40.

The Bluest Eye: A Critique of Race, Gender and Class

SHAJU NALKARA
Sree Sankaracharya University, Kalady

Toni Morrison is the first African American to win the Nobel Prize for literature in 1993, for her first novel, *The Bluest Eye*. It was written during a period of an emerging Black aesthetic, the cultural arm of the Black military movement. The novel is an incisive probe into the complex dynamics of Black self-hatred. Morrison examines how aesthetic standards derived from White culture can be detrimental to the Black people. The novel's opening lines imply the keeping of a dirty little secret, not just of personal aesthetics but of race, gender and class which prevailed at the end of the Civil Rights movement. It covers the African American experience in the mid-nineteenth century, where individuals lived in less fear but still felt the effects of social marginalization.

The novel concerns with the painful acts engaged in by and perpetrated against its Black characters, who are forced to measure themselves in terms of Western standards of beauty. This is particularly true of the Black girls and women in the novel. The now-adult Claudia MacTeer tells the story of Pecola Breedlove's destruction in a retrospective narration that recollects their childhoods. This woman as the story teller and the rememberer shares what she has seen from her Black woman's space along the periphery of the society. Her language is distinctly female, but also relies upon the performance aspects of the African-American oral tradition, the music of Gospels and the blues, and the blurring and interplay between poetry and prose.

The textual structure of *The Bluest Eye* and the construction of its characters support the woman's unique understanding and use of alternative communicative devices. Just as the novel is an extended blues lyric itself, it also tells the life of the blues lived by its women characters. Claudia's mother, Mrs. MacTeer, periodically stops talking traditional language and moves into singing the blues as she works in the kitchen, merging prose with poetry. The hard, desperate lives of the three prostitutes, China, Poland and Miss Marie are also summed up in their singing of the blues as they blur the hard lines of male language. In addition to representing the racial struggles of these characters, woman's singing also addresses gender oppression and class oppression in *The Bluest Eye.*

Mrs. MacTeer is presented as a poor, struggling Black wife and mother trying to instill a sense of pride in her daughters while pursuing the American Dream. She does not realize that by reinforcing Western ideals of beauty through the white baby dolls she gives her daughters Claudia and Frieda at Christmas, she is compromising their ability to recognize their self-worth. Morrison demonstrates Claudia's recognition of the racially selective nature of the American Dream when she depicts Claudia decapitating the white dolls and rejecting the image of Shirley Temple that everyone else, including her sister Frieda and Pecola, adores.

Pecola's experience inside the walls of the ugly storefront represents a microcosm of the violence and oppression she witnesses and experiences in the larger world. Cholly and Pauline Breedlove routinely enact for the children not scenes of love but fierce physical and verbal battles stemming from their life frustrations. Pauline rejects her own family in favour of her White employer's home and children. She is a typical mammy figure in the novel. After Cholly sets fire to their storefront home, Pecola temporarily escapes the brutal epithets that her parents inflict upon each other and their children when she moves in with the MacTeer family. Pecola drinks several quarters of milk from their home just to use their Shirley Temple mug and gaze at young Temple's blue eyes which she very much yearns for herself. However, even Mrs. MacTeer, ostensibly more motherly than Pauline, does not fail to voice, quite loudly, her discontent with the "case" who burdens the family budget by drinking so much milk. Thus even when Pecola resides with the supposedly more nurturing MacTeer family, she is in the environment that deprives her of milk, synonymous with maternal nourishment.

The three prostitutes pretend to be victorious in their battle to defeat efforts to minimize them as Black women by acting hard, by focusing on their material gains and by laughing at the men they purport to control with their sexuality. But, without uttering words in the traditional way, they demonstrate through sighs and song their failure and their regret at having to sacrifice their individual selves in order to find a place in the White man's world. These prostitutes are the outsiders in community due to their profession. But they befriend Pecola and their apartment is a haven of sorts for her. They accept her for who she is and they are the only people who make her feel beautiful and loved. They never ascend to middle-class status as a result of their associations with many of the well-to-do men of Lorain, Ohio.

The ultimate victim of the novel, Pecola, is totally lacking in self-esteem. She cannot claim power from man's language because of her femaleness; she watches and admires the bravado of the prostitutes, but finds herself unable to emulate them because of her poverty and she cannot inspire the love that the lemon-yellow Maureen Paul receives and that she so desperately wants because of her Blackness—she can never be the blonde, blue-eyed 'Mary Jane' whose face stares at her from the label of the candy she devours.

Morrison ridicules the ideal American family by showing, through the "Dick and Jane" chapter headings, that the Claudias, Friedas and Pecolas of the world are being socialized into a society which excludes them because of race, gender and class. The "Dick and Jane" primer is repeated twice. The second version closely resembles the first but is written without standard capitalization or punctuation. The third version is run together without spaces or distinction between words. Each version of the passage represents a type of family: the first version represents a

White family; the second, a struggling yet happy Black family; and the third, which has been labelled the "distorted run-on" version, represents Pecola's family.

Pecola's father, Cholly Breedlove, is used to depict the minimization of women when he is figuratively raped by a flashlight in the hand of a White man. This emasculation, with its accompanying destruction of Cholly's ability to love, is instrumental in his rape of Pecola. Innocent, passive, rejected by the White standards of society and starving for love, Pecola is the perfect sacrifice. She cannot resist this victimization because every Western ideological concept tells her that she does not have the right to resist, rather it tells her that she, as a Black and as a woman, is nobody. Her insanity brings her partial freedom because through it, she acquires 'the blue eyes' that make her acceptable to a society that places such importance and admiration on this endowment.

One of Morrison's many important contributions to African American literary history is her groundbreaking treatment of sex and sexuality. She was one of the first Black American writers to explore and depict sexuality's full spectrum of possibility, its capacity to express love, hate, joy, sadness, compassion, lust and even longing for spiritual transcendence. For her, sex is as much a part of life, as birth and death. She treats it in the same way that she approaches all aspects of human relationship without sentiment or censure. Her treatment of sexuality locates her in the larger historical context of Black American history.

The novel details the psychological disintegration of Pecola after she is raped by her father. Morrison deliberately broke the taboo of speaking openly about such a dark issue, as she insisted on producing fiction that described every aspect of the Black community including good and bad experiences. The author presents rape in the novel as symptomatic of American race relations. Pecola's rape is partly the result of her father, Cholly, having been "raped" by White men when he was a teenager. These men surprise Cholly while he is having sex with a girl in the woods and then force him at gun point to continue the act. Morrison tells us that Cholly hated the girl who was his sexual partner because she had witnessed his failure and that he later transfers this shame and hatred to Pecola, another girl whom he cannot protect from the destructive forces of a racist American society.

The Black characters in the novel appear to act violently towards other Blacks. The self-proclaimed spiritualist and psychic, Micah Elihue Whitcomb, alias Soaphead Church, ministers to the people through false promises and services his own needs by molesting little girls. He considers both his ministry and molestations as ordained by God and that they are expressions of God's love through him. Pecola is obsessed by the idea that only people with blue eyes can ever be truly beautiful. She is misled by Soaphead Church when she comes to him with the request for blue eyes. As a result she metaphorically blinds herself in an attempt to conform to this idea. Despite his earlier crimes against the community and his inability to see its ugliness, he genuinely empathizes with Pecola. He knows that she is in search of the thing that all the people he meets, including himself, desire—she wants to be loved. His pervasions illuminate the pervasions of a world driven by race as a determinant of love. We find his endeavours loathsome. He himself is a product of inbreeding and incest. Like everyone else, he abuses Pecola's need and uses her desperation to help alleviate a nuisance in his own life.

Pecola's rape by her father, the death of her child whom she conceived as a result of the rape, compounded with Soaphead's trickery and the community's abuse, causes Pecola to spiral into madness. In her madness, Soaphead leaves her with the belief that she has blue eyes. In his own madness, he chastises God in a letter for not bestowing upon Pecola the one thing she desires. He assigns a level of greatness to his own person in his ability to give her and other little girls, the love that they want, the love that he himself is denied. Ultimately, he becomes not just a critique of the world but a critique of how the world justifies who and what it loves.

In explaining Pecola's descent to insanity, Morrison explains why such tragedies occur. In her desire for blue eyes that she associates with beauty and acceptance, Pecola sets herself up for disappointment. As she details this loss, Morrison exposes how the culture in which Pecola lives creates the false standards of beauty she strives for and how these standards lead her to ultimate doom. The Black's feeling of inferiority is the result of the values of America's White patriarchal system which treats and perceives Blacks as objects of contempt. Pecola embraces this value system along with the consequent sense of inferiority that stems from dominant racial stereotypes and Whites' projection of racist shame.

There is no figure in *The Bluest Eye* who ascends from darkness and emerges into the light, who finds enlightenment and chooses it over the shadow. In Pauline Breedlove and the sugar-brown Mobile girls we find the unwillingness to step outside of the cave, when they are given the opportunity, an unwillingness driven by fear and a need to exist within a false, albeit familiar, construct because it is comfortable and safe rather than emerge from the cave and face the painful light of the sun. Most of the characters in the novel are thus internally colonized. Through the character of Pecola, Morrison investigates how a vulnerable child internalizes and embraces damaging racial stereotypes with the potential to destroy her. Pecola's displacement leaves her with no place to go or to grow. Just as the marigolds die because Claudia plants them too deep, Pecola cannot blossom because she finds herself planted in non-nurturing soil.

The Black community in *The Bluest Eye* is envisaged as existing like a cell within the larger white body of America, sustained by traditional strengths and values but being weakened by divisions within it. These divisions are the result of a complicated process of Black people's adjustment and accommodation to white norms. In the novel, whiteness appears not as a racial category but as the norm against which all other races are measured. Whiteness appears here as an ideal rather than a race.

The story does not end with Pecola's destruction, however. Morrison salvages the Black woman by designating Claudia as the voice of survival. It is the story coming from Claudia that redeems the Black woman in the end. Morrison sums up Pecola's fate and the novel's powerful theme:

> The damage done was total. She spent her days, her tendril, sap-green days, walking up and down, up and down, her head jerking to the beat of a drummer so distant only she could hear. Elbows bent, hands on shoulders, she flailed her arms like a bird in an eternal, grotesquely futile effort to fly. Beating the air, a winged but grounded bird, intent on the blue void it could not reach—could not even see—but which filled the valleys of the mind. (162)

We are led to conclude that the narrator, Claudia MacTeer and her sister Frieda probably dodged this pervasion by directing an inordinate malice at their Shirley Temple dolls and by being born to a family that, though rough and austere, did know how to breed love unlike the Breedloves who are unable to do so, in contradiction to the meanjng of their name. Claudia tries to understand her own involvement in Pecola's tragedy as the narrative also seeks to explain why a father in the ironically named Breedlove family should impregnate his own daughter.

Every element of Morrison's text has its counter text. The notion of "the bluest eye," for example, suggests that her primary concern is with the culture's standard of beauty. This is evident in Claudia's observation towards the end of the novel:

> All of us—all who knew her—felt so wholesome after we cleaned ourselves on her. We were so beautiful when we stood astride her ugliness. Her simplicity decorated us, her guilt sanctified us, her pain made us glow with health, her awkwardness made us think we had a sense of humour. Her inarticulateness made us believe we were eloquent. Her poverty kept us generous. (163)

Claudia conceives of the world in terms of race alone when she deconstructs white dolls. Eventually, she learns to have the regard for those dolls that her parents have. She understands the limitations of her perspective. She recognizes that due to her femaleness and economic status, she is subject to the same social forces moulding others. Her experience demonstrates that in a land where the bluest eye holds hegemony, none of the dispossessed escapes its gaze.

The novel inscribes identification in terms of fantasy while reversing the movement from Black to White and exposing both the cultural construction of racial difference and the harrowing effects to which it gives rise. In these ways, identification—whether from Black to White or White to Black—emerges as a complex, highly charged and multi-faceted phenomenon, linking the violent histories of slavery, colonialism and racial oppression by which they are traversed. They are sights of political struggle and friction; the crossings of identification constitute spaces in others where psychic and historic realities, the subjective and the ideological, dramatically collide. Thus, her novels have created space for Black and feminist texts, changing the overwhelming male makeup of the African American literary canon.

Works Cited

Morrison, Toni. *The Bluest Eye*. London: Picador, 1990.

Peach, Linden. *Toni Morrison*. New York: St. Martin's Press, 2000.

Thody, Philip. *Twentieth-Century Literature: Critical Issues and Themes*. London: Macmillan, 1996.

Denial of Woman's Personality in *The Bluest Eye*: A Psychoanalytical Study

SHAIL BALA
Res. Sch., Jai Prakash University, Chapra (Bihar)

During the 1970s, we come across a great and grand creative urge coming out from the art and mind of Toni Morrison. "As a novelist, she explores all the dimensions and dynamics of relationship to ponder over it comparatively to the western parameters of women's beauty and the socio-psychological suppression of Black community particularly of the woman. *The Bluest Eye* saw the light in 1970 and the centrality of this novel is designed around the obsession of blacks with an American measurement of beauty. In fact it has become almost impossible to desert and denounce the American mode of determination in connection with beauty. The novel is a traumatic tale of a black girl's search to obtain white parameters. In American parameter of beauty, blue eyes, blonde hair and white skin are the requisite elements and ingredients to fathom the charm and grace of a woman. *The Bluest Eye* traces the painful condition of blacks especially women in America where till date racial consideration commands everything. The American society boasts of the development of individuality irrespective of race and gender. Traditionally, the African American society has been witnessing excesses and atrocities perpetrated against them by the whites and Morrison makes a thorough inquiry of this peculiar state. In her thought-provoking survey, Toni Morrison receives disrupted emotions which came out from "living in a world where white standards and goals are presented to blacks as uniquely important and, at the same time, impossible for them to achieve".[2] The entire story rotates around Pecola Breedlove, the young black girl who is of the mind that blackness condemns her to ugliness and lovelessness. This is not the singular consideration of the novelist, rather she justifies it by exposing the ugliness of black poverty, powerlessness and loss of pragmatic and assertive conception of 'self 'and being.

The Bluest Eye unearths that racism is hazardous to the self-image of the African society in general and the black female in particular. The novel gives the pricking story of Pecola who comes of a poor family detached from the mainstream of life of a community. The Breedloves cultivate hatred against themselves and they believe that they have translated their unworthiness into ugliness. No doubt, woman as a creature is the precious creation of Almighty. It is realised that the body of woman is one of the essential elements in her situation in the world, but the body is not enough to define her as a woman."[3] In American context, the concept of blackness has been held as an unfavorable connotation in the popular mind. There are numerous phrases and proverbs designed by the people with nefarious intention like 'black is evil', 'black as sin', 'black as the devil' which reflect the emotional and aesthetic implications. The evil and ugliness of blackness have been presented and denoted like antithesis of the goodness and sanity of whiteness. It has almost acquired moral connotation. In order to establish the holy domination, "the black race was by nature incapable of freedom and marked out for slavery."[4] It has been clarified by a French diplomat and anthropologist Count Joseph Arthur De Gobineau, "I have no hesitation in regarding the white race as superior to all others in beauty. . . . Human groups are unequal in beauty, and this inequality is racial, logical, permanent and indestructible."[5]

The narrative pattern of *The Bluest Eye* is classified into four sections and each section is named after a season, which begins with autumn and closes with summer. The story starts with a reference from Dick and Jane Primer taught to American children and printed in three ways. It is first printed in a common way, afterwards without capitalization and punctuation and also without any spaces given between words. There is a description of a happy white American family which is meant to provide an ironic epigraph to the whole narrative design. Hence, there is an introductory message put forward by Claudia MacTeer, a girl child who grows to adulthood and narrates the fictive set-up. It should ever be in mind that the plot-structure of *The Bluest Eye* is diametrically different from Tolstoy's philosophy as he believes and practises in the *War and Peace* like Rise-Fall-Rise. The narrator makes us alarmingly aware of how Pecola got herself pregnant by her own father, Cholly Breedlove and lost her child in miscarriage. Meanwhile, Claudia and her sister played an important role for the safe birth of the child but in vain. Each section of the novel begins with Claudia speaking in her own voice and giving us some of Pecola's life or story that she has come across. At times, we notice that there are other voices as well. Pecola hails from an underdog and unprivileged family that is actually dissociated from the usual current of life of a community. The Breedloves develop disdain against themselves as they become the victim of their own inability. Pecola's mother Pauline who works in the capacity of maid-servant in a beautiful house does not like and approve the abject condition and ugliness of her house, her daughter, her family and herself. Genuinely, she hates poverty and blackness. The novel becomes a saga or a mythical document that denotes human potency and explains the viable greatness of the people who are suppressed by the idea that they are outsiders. The novel makes it a point of discourse how Pecola is compelled to aspire for blue eyes like those of white children. She has immense urge to be loved and identified by both whites and blacks. The white standard of beauty becomes a key-point in the mind of Pecola's dream and desire. The racist idea of physical beauty in the novel controls and captures the narrativity and leads straight to Pecola's painful suffering. The novelist goes to the extent of saying that the equating of physical beauty with virtue is the pernicious and destructive idea of the western world. The physical glamour has nothing to do with our past, present and time to come. To her, it also damages one's self-image and further destroys happiness and throttles creativity. Apparently, colour-consciousness is a perpetuating presence in the novel and along with it the economic status has a decisive influence on how the dynamics of relationships should be viewed and reviewed. Pecola who never finds herself graceful is infatuated for the eyes of the whites what she intends to get through miracle. Truly, she is obsessed with the physical attractions of the white and the novelist in this connection elegantly explores her mind: "When the strength of a race depends on its beauty, when the focus is turned to how one looks as opposed to what one is, we are in trouble."[6]

Of course, Pecola does not identify it as she is mesmerised of white cultural notion. She faces very brutal form of negligence and rejection. Her parents never experienced the fruit of love so they were unable to provide the worth of love. These all things crystallize owing to racial impiety. In the early section of the novel, the racial predicament comes to fore and focus. The simple cauterization of the novel like autumn manifests in a way that the fictive universe is badly disturbed. Spring normally stands for the beginning of things, the time of birth and rebirth. Almost in contrast winter is the embodiment of decay and death. Moreover, summer suggests life in charm and maturity which also leads towards death. Critically speaking, the classification according to seasons underlines the understanding and the natural dislocation of life of the Africans residing in the United States. Toni Morrison has provided the three sets of language signifying three life-styles. The first form of narration suggests an alienated white world represented by the Dick-Jane family that comes to the lives of the black children. Morrison shows the simplicity in the first set of her expression.

> Here is the house. It is green and white. It has a red door. It is very pretty. Here is the family. Mother, Father, Dick and Jane live in the green-and-white house. They are very happy. See Jane. She has a red dress. She wants to play. Who will play with Jane? . . . Look, look. Here comes a friend. The friend will play with Jane. They will play a good game. Play, Jane, play.[7] (1)

The second set embodies the life-style of the MacTeer family which signifies the poverty and the racism that it combats in Ohio. The second section repeats the same passage exactly but has no capital letters and punctuation. The third section offers distorted running version of the paragraph symbolising the Breedlove family which resides in a deformed universe being exploited by the ruling class.

The novelist explored her motive for *The Bluest Eye* in an interview. She says: "In *The Bluest Eye* I use the Primer story, with its picture of the happy family, as a frame acknowledging the outer civilisation. The Primer with white children was the way of life presented to the black people. As the novel proceeded I wanted that Primer version broken up and confused, which explains the typographical running together of the words."[8]

Morrison suggests another innovation by selecting a woman point of view from which the fiction is narrated and examined. There is an appropriate comparison between *Huckleberry Finn* and *The Bluest Eye* which brings forth the different narrative strategy advocated by Toni Morrison. Mark Twain shows a white boy who seeks the full humanity of a black adult. In doing so the novelist focuses the inherited prejudices. But Toni Morrison modifies the paradigm and selects a very young black girl who is an observer-participant in the fiction and she becomes the principal narrator. It is true that the destructive myth of white beauty is astonishingly suggestive to women. Claudia does not have the same fate as we find in case of Pecola. She is a bit younger than Pecola and both of them got their education in the same school. For a few days, Pecola enjoys the company of MacTeers. Actually, Claudia is not the singular voice of the novel. Morrison adopts a strategy in which there is a third person narrator who fulfils the vacuum created by Claudia. The third person omniscient narrator gives the information about the Breedloves, Geraldine and her family. Another striking feature of Morrison's narrativity suggests, albeit *The Bluest Eye* is a search novel, the fictionalist does not show the intensity of mission and motive. Claudia's narrative technique starts at the end by synthesizing the traumatic conclusion of Pecola's life. In a suggestive note, it is Claudia who matures into adult—she speaks about the failure of her and her sister's endeavour to make Pecola's baby live through the use of the magical incantation and the disintegration of the Breedlove family. She also argues the motive of the narrative. "There is really nothing more to say—except why. But since why is always difficult to handle, one must take refuge in how."

The cyclic characteristic of Claudia's narrative approach is also approved by the different seasons. The narrative device of Morrison is very similar to E.M. Forster's in *A Passage to India*. But Forster differs from her in the realm of meaning and message as he becomes philosopher but she remains only a realist. The narrative cycling starts with the autumn and finishes with summer. The ironic situation is that Pecola's story is not the normal discourse of birth, death and rebirth from planting to harvest to planting, rather it is a story that moves from pathos to tragedy and finally to madness. Claudia's mode of narration confirms ripeness that is making an effort to recall or recapture her past experience. Just like the deliberation of Henry Vaughan in *The Retreat*, Claudia makes a jump from childhood to young age, then vice-versa. She becomes nostalgic and the entire past is before her eyes. The simplicity of her memory is reflected and she very limpidly but gracefully depicts the entire episode as if one who knows what will happen next and what she will or will not understand. She goes ahead with this kind of tone for three pages. The entire exploration is dense with concretized details which are very much fixed on the mind of a child of nine. It suggests that Claudia is inclined to give more than her narration. She also talks of a debate that Pecola's life is more important than the cause and effect phenomenon. This points out the fragmented narratology of the novel. The novelist is vigilant of the role of class considerations, particularly in the minor families. She frequently talks about the inter-racial preoccupations based on the colour of the skin rather than the class oriented form. The principal focus in *The Bluest Eye* is on colour-discrimination faced by the African people. The numerous incidents take place in the heart of the novel which pushed Pecola into oblivion. She has acquired awesome realization when she encounters an old white storekeeper. Not only has she been teased by the whites but also by the black boys at school.

The other side of the thematic exploration is equally pricking when Pecola's mother also offers her tender and sympathetic feeling to her employer's children who are, no doubt, white people. Psychoanalytically, the blacks are so depressed that they do not even spare the blacks. This is the white yardstick which has polluted the heart and mind of the black people. Consequently, they have become victims of self-hatred. The novelist says: "It was as though some mysterious all-knowing master has given each one a cloak of ugliness to wear, and they had each accepted it without question. The master had said, 'you are ugly people.' They looked about themselves and saw nothing to contradict the statement, saw, in fact, support for it leaning at them from every billboard, every mood, every glance." (28)

The heart-rending scene of cruelty and crime for Pecola comes to light when we visualize the scene of rape by her own father, Cholly. This was really an inhuman and unnatural act of physical assault. Here Cholly comes to Pecola with the intention to liberate her from the bond of loveless situation. But suddenly he comes into the grip of lust and fails to seize his temptation. It is a distortion and dehumanization of fatherly love. Afterwards, Pecola conceives; her still-born child symbolizes the slavery and suffocation of her life. Pecola is surrounded by problems and puzzlements where she is not only a scapegoat for her parents but also for the mulattos. Claudia, the narrator of the novel, also presents her as a scapegoat:

> All of us—all who knew herself so wholesome after we cleaned ourselves on her. We were so beautiful when we stood astride her ugliness. Her simplicity decorated us, her guilt sanctified us, her pain made us glow with health, her awkwardness made us think we had a sense of humour. Her inarticulateness made us generous. With her waking dreams we used to silence our own nightmares. And she let us and thereby deserved our contempt. We honed our egos on her, padded our characters with her frailty and yawned in the fantasy of our strength." (163)

The narrator of the novel is of the opinion that Pecola herself is responsible for her destiny and character. In the novel, sex and love are principal preoccupations. Since Claudia is recalling her childhood days with Pecola, we have an eyewitness detail of their curiosity and their fears about menstruation, pregnancy and also what love is. The awakening of children to their sexuality and later to love is a natural part of the process of maturity and the achievement of selfhood. What complicates the process is the fact that the three children with whom the novel is centrally concerned are surrounded by the powerful parameters of white behaviour. The novelist goes into the heart and psyche of the blacks residing in the white society. In fact, the black woman makes her best effort to channelise her romantic passion with what she has acquired from white movies. The power of love can also be spoiled owing to the viciousness and insensitivity of the American white society. Death of romantic love on the one hand and the distortion of love on the other lead to serious consequences for the psychic health of the individuals and damage their ability to relate to one another in a positive manner. Apart from it, the novelist puts an emphasis on the quality of sex, life and marriage. Pauline's marriage with Cholly is full of puzzlements but the memory of fulfilling sex with him in the earlier days of marriage haunts her. She feels as if he were 'laughing between my legs' and as if 'it be rainbow all inside.' This shows that Pecola has received disturbed parentage which has aggravated her trauma. She behaves abnormally, thinking that her eyes have acquired blue colour. These things culminate due to the racist and sexist culture prevalent in the society. Shelby Steel rightly suggests: "to be black was to be a victim, therefore, not to be a victim was not to be a black."[9] The mental state of Pecola has rightly been described thus: "She believes that exchanging her brown eyes for blue ones will make her beautiful. The people who influence Pecola as she grows up are clearly the source for this harmful idea. As appearance approved by dominant white society, such people damage both themselves and others."[10] There is a Shirley Temple doll with which the girls play who possesses blue eyes. Moreover, the little daughter of the employer of Pecola's mother has blue eyes. She however believes that getting the blue eyes will provide some significant dimension to her personality. In that case, she may command love and security which she is missing at present. She feels blue eyes will prove a bliss and panacea for all the ailments: "it had occurred to Pecola sometime ago if her eyes . . . were different . . . she herself would be different. . . . If she looked different, beautiful, maybe (her father) would be different and (her mother) too. Maybe they'd say, why look at pretty-eyed Pecola. We must not do bad things in front of those pretty eyes."

However, it can be said that the blue eyes are treated to be the symbol of myth. It has been broadly realised and remarked that the possession of blue eyes embodies the attainment of everything like love, recognition, identity, entity, friends and family—which finally establish the individual in the society. The novelist has symbolically offered the white baby dolls which have been discussed at length by Claudia, the narrator. She says, "Adults, older girls, shops, magazines, newspaper, window signs—all the world had agreed that a blue eyed, yellow-haired, pink-skinned doll was what every girl treasured."[14] Even for the parents, dolls stand for unfulfilled desires of their own childhood. Pecola's mother Pauline suffers consciously or unconsciously from the colour-complex which is inherited by Pecola. She comes under the awesome feeling of vulgarity compared to the little white girl who seems to represent her community that is only correct. The most striking aspect of Pauline's personality that she has developed is a tortured self of despising herself. She is fully vigilant of the changing wheels of racial torture in her life but she makes no attempt to prevent it. Pauline plays a delightful role in several realms and respects. She also works as surrogate mother for Fisher's young daughter, Polly. She gets significance at the house of Fisher's family only because of her service and devotion to the white people. Here we come across Pauline and the conventional black mammy. It should be kept in mind that the black mother is very significant almost in all the white American fictions. This is simply because the black women are much serviceable, punctual, duty-bond and loyal to their work and responsibility.

Jacques Lacan propounds the theory of Mirror Stage to argue the origin and development of the concerned persons. The idea of image is noticeable in the process of recognizing one's self. At the same time, it enables to realise the identification of another as a significant fact. Lacan is of the view that identification is a matter of searching and locating the concept of beauty on the levels of formative and erogenic. No doubt, the correlation of beauty to sexual and social fulfilment suggests a priority of thought for Morrison. Like a psychoanalyst, Toni Morrison advocates the anxiety of black women—what they feel after observing mirrors as they live in the white dominated society. The mirror reflects the cultural or patriarchal image of the black women in their introspection. It also gives a painful idea that they are not properly women in the conventional sense. That's why Pecola used to pass "long hours . . . looking in the mirror, time to discover the secret of the ugliness, that made her ignored or despised." (39) It is a matter of probing that Pecola is not running after white beauty but facing an existential crisis: what beauty really symbolises. Sartre says: "we are condemned to be free." The simple implication is that every individual intends to look beautiful; if one does not get the expected desire, one becomes the victim of complex. In *The Bluest Eye*, Lacan's theory of the mirror stage is quite applicable. For Pecola, an approving mirror is similar to an approving mother. Winnicott finds the child looking upon the mother's face in order to locate himself/herself: "In other words, the mother is looking at the baby and what she looks like is related to what she sees there."[11]

The bitterness of Pecola's suffering comes out not only from the racism but also gives inter-racial conflicts in relation to colour deeply rooted in white racist myths. Pecola promotes a positive sense of being when she watches the values of light-skinned Maureen Peal whose sense of greatness is attached to her colour. Morrison is very much incisive in her argument when she says how the Breedloves' appearance emerges to be problem-ridden. It is not their ugliness, but their conviction of their ugliness that points out the real difference. Pecola notes the irreparable damage received from inter-racial preoccupation. It is a matter of examination on the part of the child when Pauline at the time of Pecola's birth says that she is an ugly child. The child, however, loses its sense of worth if it finds the mother mirror controlled only by moods or worse still, the rigidity of her defences. From the very inception of the novel, Pauline Breedlove works as a mirror and reflects to her daughter her own sense of inferiority which enters Pecola and she radiates it back to her. The critic says, "This mother-daughter mirror reflects images of sometimes-self and sometime-other in their struggle to know who each is, an effort which runs generationally. The reverence for whiteness, which is Pecola's most valued possession, is passed on to Pauline through the intergenerational mirror by her mother. Pauline seeks her own missing mother as she looks at Pecola."[12] Pauline once tells Pecola, "so when I seed it [the baby] it was like looking at a picture of your mama when she was a girl. You know who she is, but she does not look the same." (99) It should be remembered that Pauline's mother works as a maid to white family. The intergenerational mirror has already punctured Pauline's mental condition and put her beyond redemption. She does not accept any concept of internal wholeness based on cultural liberty by thinking that freedom will come from outside. Pauline comes to the dream world of white under the impression that she has got sophistication but the harsh reality is that she is suffering from psychological ailment. The in-depth socio-psychological observation reveals the fact that Pecola's suffering is based on the failure of her family which does not offer proper kind of socialization, education, love and sense of security which are requisite for the healthier growth of the child. Parents cannot be changed and for Pecola it is bad luck because she did not get good parentage. In addition, she suffers from the feeling of self-hatred because of her colour-complex. Morrison argues that Pecola's sense of alienation and unworthiness come to the front and focus not because of the others' approach; these culminate owing to her own failure and incompetency to cope with the situation.

Pauline and Pecola suffer because of the oppressive and exploitative nature of an American yardstick of female beauty. The enemy of their inhuman suffering is not simply a single man either black or white; the fiercest enemy is the dominant majority culture which has perpetuated the oppressive yardstick in every respect. Toni Morrison does not pronounce the political feminism which alienates black women from the black men but a more self-conscious appreciation of the particular beauty of black women. It is, however, not the physical parameter of beauty that these later women feel most oppressed by the society but these are their roles and character, which make them victim. Morrison genuinely makes a vigorous attack against racism. *The Bluest Eye* identifies the unnatural position of blacks in a society ruled by colour and sex. She all the time poses a greater question of 'being' through the characters of the novel. The most important thing is that every individual is eager and inclined to accept the responsibility for his/her own life. Lawrence goes into the different layers of meaning and suggests: "Morrison is concerned with the ontological structures and mythological thought system that blacks developed reinforce their definition of self and existence."[13] The black women moreover find themselves in a double crunch of race and gender. There is a kind of pressure on the individual to leave her individuality and cultural entity and to follow the white dictates. The novelist seemingly makes an inquiry into Pecola's life on the axis of race and gender. Morrison is herself of the opinion that "the assertion of racial beauty was not a reaction to the self-mocking, humorous critique of cultural racial foibles common in all groups, but against the damaging internalization of assumptions of immutable inferiority originating in an outside gaze. The novel tried to hit the raw nerve of racial self-contempt, expose it, then soothe it not with narcotics but with the language that replicated the agency I discovered in my first experience of beauty."

The Bluest Eye proposes a black girlhood when it seeks identity-image from white culture and from the malevolent parental mirror. In the fashion of Paule Marshal and others, Morrison shows her belief in the angst and agony of the black women and girls about what their mirrors suggest them. Maud Martha, a character of Gwendolyn Brooks demonstrates her sense of reality and she tries to search herself from the viewpoint of her husband . . . it's my colour that makes him mad. I try to shut my eyes to that, but it's no good. What I am inside. What is really me, he likes okay. But he keeps looking at my colour—which is like a wall. He has to jump over it in order to meet and touch what I've got for him. He has to jump away up high in order to see it. He gets awful tired of that jumping."[14]

Morrison emphatically argues that the African American women are badly affected by the sexist and racist constrictions of the society. There is a close relationship between sex and race and it is quite natural for the black women to focus the self-felt experience. Here, women experience as women in socio-psychological context. There is a popular saying in the west "Tota mulier in Utero" (woman is nothing but a womb) which is aptly applicable to the narrative art of Morrison. The novelist is under the impression that there are certain things which can be experienced only by women. Raman Selden rightly suggests, "Since only women, the argument goes, have undergone those specifically female life-experiences (ovulation, menstruation, parturition), only they can speak of a woman's life. Further, a woman's experience includes a different perceptual and emotional life; women do not see things in the same ways as men, and have different ideas and feelings about what is important or not important."[15]

In the second category of women, Morrison talks about the sugar-brown mobile girl living in better neighbourhood where there are privilege and facilities. These women have smooth hands and slim ankles. No doubt, they marry and beget children but to them sex is repulsive. In schools and colleges, they have been taught how to do the white men's work with refinement, how to instruct black children in obedience and how to develop thrift, patience, high morals and good manners. The theme of the novel is mind-boggling and thought-provoking. All the time, socio-cultural construct determines the sexual and behavioural pattern of the society. Raman Selden says, "in the earlier phase of women feminist writing on literature [Kate Millett, Germaine Greer, Mary Ellmann] the emphasis was often quite political in the sense that the writers were expressing angry feelings of injustice and were engaged in raising women's political awareness of their oppression by men. . . . Unlike blacks, women are not a minority, and unlike a proletariat, women are not a product of history."[16]

The third type of women that Morrison discusses in the novel bear no desire for prosperity of rootedness. Here, Morrison differs from Simon de Beauvoir because the French philosopher does not believe in the categorization of women as Karl Marx has done. To Morrison, there are prostitutes and embittered women who have developed hatred for all the men without any discretion and rationality. To such women, everything is a subject of denunciation and depravity. This is all because of patriarchal frame of mind. Kate Millett's *Sexual Politics* offers an analysis of the patriarchal culture. In fact, Millett and Shulamith Firestone (*The Dialectic of Sex* 1972) are of the opinion that male-domination is primary and it is quite independent of other's social and economic forms of oppression. Like Morrison, Firestone's theoretical purpose is to substitute sex for class as the primal historical determination. Indubitably, the concept of class struggle is itself a result of the organization of the biological family unit. To Mitchell Barrett, patriarchy and capitalism oversimplify a complex process. These two exercised the economic organisation of households and its accompanying familial ideology, the division of labour in the economic system, the systems of education and states, the cultural processes where men and women are differently represented. We find the nature of gender identity and the relationship between sexuality and biological reproduction. Virginia Woolf says that the condition under which men and women produce literature are materially different and influenced the form and feature of their creative urge. One cannot separate the problem of gender from material conditions in history. In Morrison, the ideology of gender influences the mode of creative enterprise of men and women.

Morrison believes that economics plays a decisive role in the exploitation of African people. In Shakespeare's *Othello* also, the protagonist becomes the victim of racism. The hero is unable to sort out the problems of his familial life. Time and again, he has been abused and attacked merely in the name of colour or race and finally tragedy takes place. Emily Bronte offers a subdued and subjugated position to the protagonist Heathcliff. He can be a soul mate, an eternal rock but he cannot be a husband of Catherine because he is black and is socially marginalized. Calvin Hernton analyses the socio-psychological framework of the society and argues: "racism is a man-made, man-enforced phenomenon . . . may be defined as all of the learned behaviour and learned emotions on the part of the group of people towards another group whose physical characteristics are dissimilar to the formal group, behaviour and emotion that compel one group to conceive of and to treat the other on the basis of its physical characteristics alone, as if it did not belong to the human race."[17]

The overriding tenet and treatment of the novel is controlled by the philosophy of racism and sexism from which the black society suffers. Kenneth Clark says: "the basic myth of racism is that white-skinned colour brings with it superiority that the white is more intelligent and virtuous."[18] The depiction of black women in Toni Morrison's fiction resists a glorified and heroic status. A critic rightly comments, "the text though seems to be referring to the feminine way of Pauline's fight, actually it says that it is not so by labeling Cholly a 'coward' and his opponent, here Pauline 'a man'. Here wife fights like a man whereas the husband fights like a coward using no weapon except his hands whereas the women uses flat iron. So Pauline is 'manly' and Cholly is 'feminine'."[19] It is actually a kind of destruction and reconstruction of the image advocated by Aristotle, Charles Darwin and others. The textual strategy of Morrison confirms that there is always another side to the coin. The text suggests a different dimension to the personality of Pauline which also problematises the reading flavour. The biological division inflicted upon different shades of emotions and experiences don't cut much ice. However, the tone and pitch for a critical attitude and the questioning frame of mind is determined by Morrison's fiction which seems to be more valuable and result-oriented than any other kind of creative exploration. The narrative world of Morrison belongs to the broad view of art for social purpose. She like G.B. Shaw and Tolstoy emerges to be a social reformer but her writing is not like a propaganda. Her creative effort creates a ripple and literary sensation among intellectually and culturally excited and vigilant people. She discusses both passive and active realism. There is a note of sad and sordid reality but she is full of optimism and hope. She inspires every reader to think hopefully and beautifully. "Passive and active realism can both serve a social purpose. But passive realism often preaches fatalism, pessimism and uselessness of endeavours to improve society. Active realism, by contrast, is optimistic, characterized by its solicitude and concern for the people inspiring them to strive against their plight and improve their social conditions."[20]

Morrison is truthful to the cause of women and she is also hyper-sensitive towards political thinking, culture, critical theory and above all humanism. In broader perspective, Morrison's novels are documents of the dynamics of human relationship. The French feminist thinker Helene Cixous suggests the idea of ecriture feminine in which she specified the fact that on the basis of writing there can be a critical trace of the points like feminine in theme, style and approach and altogether away from Phallogocentric feature. Toni Morrison's narrative art is an exact case from this point of view though the European social structure is a bit different from African American; the case of women is almost the same irrespective of country and continent. Like Sandra Gilbert and Susan Gubar's *The Mad Woman in the Attic* (1979), Morrison makes a significant assessment by exploring, exposing and redefining the position of women in the socio-historical, political and economic context, highlighting her latent power and talent. She strongly shows her disrespect to patriarchal society which nourishes preoccupied notion of women being synonymous with womb, bust and hips. Morrison's treatment becomes different from others because she is committed to the black women's experiences.

NOTES

1. Qtd. *The Hindu*, Magazine, Sunday, August 24, 2008, 5.
2. Elizabeth Janeway, *Women's Literature* (New York: Hoffman 1979), 383.

3. Seyla Benhabib and Drucilla Cornell, *Feminism as Critique: Essay on the Politics of Gender in Late Capitalist Society* (Oxford: Polity Press, 1987), 134.
4. John Stuart Mill, "The Subjection of Women," *On Liberty and the Subjection of Women* (Hertfordshire: Wordsworth Classics, 1996), 127.
5. Qtd. Donald B. Gibson, "Text and Counter-Text in *The Bluest Eye*," *Toni Morrison: Critical Perspectives Past and Present*, ed. Henry Louis Gates Jr. et al. (New York: Amistad, 1993), 159.
6. Toni Morrison, "Behind the Making of the Black Book," *Black World*, 23 (1974), 89.
7. Toni Morrison, *The Bluest Eye* (London, Vintage, 1999).
8. Thomas LeClair, "The Language Must Not Sweat: A Conversation with Toni Morrison", *Toni Morrison: Critical Perspectives Past and Present*, ed. Henry Louis Gates Jr. and K.A. Appiah, 376.
9. Steel Shelby, "Black Consciousness in Perspective," *The American Review*, 33, 1 (1989), 58.
10. Elizabeth B. House, "Artists and the Art of Living: Order and Disorder in Toni Morrison's Fiction," *Modern Fiction Studies*, 34, 1 (1988), 29.
11. Harihar Kulkarni, "Mirrors, Reflections and Images: Malady of Generational Relationship and Girlhood in Toni Morrison's *The Bluest Eye*, *Indian Journal of American Studies*, 23, 3 (Summer 1993), 1.
12. *Ibid.*, 2.
13. Hogue Lawrence, *Discourse and the Other* (Durham: Duke University Press, 1986), 133.
14. Gwendolyn Brooks, *Maud Martha* (New York: Harper, 1953), 87.
15. Raman Selden, *A Reader's Guide to Contemporary Literary Theory* (The Harvester Press, 1985), 130.
16. *Ibid.*, 132.
17. Calvin Hernton, *Sex and Racism in America* (New York: Grove, 1965), 175.
18. Kenneth Clark, *Black and White: The Ghetto Inside* (Lapides and Burrows, 1971), 104-20.
19. R.K. Dhawan, ed., *Feminism and American Literature* (New Delhi: Prestige, 1996), 103.
20. M. Katju, "The true role of art and literature," *The Hindu* (New Delhi, August 18, 2008), 11.